The

Discus

An Owner's Guide To

A HAPPY HEALTHY FISH

Howell Book House

IDG Books Worldwide, Inc.
An International Data Group Company
Foster City, CA • Chicago, IL • Indianapolis, IN • New York, NY • Southlake, TX

Howell Book House
IDG Books Worldwide, Inc.
An International Data Group Company
919 E. Hillsdale Boulevard
Suite 400
Foster City, CA 94404

The IDG Books Worldwide logo is a registered trademark under exclusive license to IDG Books Worldwide, Inc., from International Data Group, Inc.

For general information on IDG Books Worldwide's books in the U.S., please call our Consumer Customer Service department at 800-762-2974. For reseller information, including discounts and premium sales, please call our Reseller Customer Service department at 800-434-3422.

Library of Congress Cataloging-in-Publication Data
Hargrove, Mic.
The discus : an owner's guide to happy healthy fish / [Mic Hargrove, Maddy Hargrove, David Brown].
p.   cm.
Includes bibliographical references.
ISBN: 1-58245-112-5
1. Discus (Fish)   I. Hargrove, Maddy.   II. Brown, David.   III. Title.
SF458.D5H27   1999
639.3'774—dc21   99-34072
                                      CIP
Manufactured in the United States of America

10 9 8 7 6 5 4 3 2 1

Series Director: Amanda Pisani, Nikki Moustaki
Book Design: Michele Laseau
Cover Design: Iris Jeromnimon
Illustration: Laura Robbins
Photography: All photography, including front and back cover, by Aaron Norman
Production Team: Linda Quigley, Holly Wittenberg, Donna Wright

The fishes photographed for this book were provided by Victor Hritz of the Crystal Aquarium, Marc Weiss of World Wide Fish Farms, William Appel and David Weber.

Contents

All
About

part one

Discus

External Features of the Discus

Eye

Mouth

Gill Cover

Pelvic Fin

Dorsal Fin

Caudal Fin

Anal Fin

chapter 1

The **King** of the **Amazon**

I can think of no greater joy than owning an aquarium. Tropical fish lend a special healing power to the everyday problems and stress that we all have to manage. An aquarium is therapeutic, educational and fun. Although all aquarium fish are beautiful and interesting in their own right, once in a while a certain species comes along and completely captures our imagination and desire.

Love at First Sight

I cannot truly describe the enchantment that I felt when I first laid eyes upon a discus. Its large dancing eyes captured my heart and enthralled me to no end. I knew at that moment, that I just had to have one of these beautiful and graceful fish in my home aquarium. A discus is very similar in nature to a family's dog. This species of fish will recognize its owner and swim joyfully to the surface to help him greet the beginning of each new day. Fascinating moments like these make aquarium keeping one of the most popular and most cherished hobbies in the world.

The King of the Amazon

Many consider the discus to be the undisputed "king" of all tropical aquarium fish. Few other fish display the natural beauty, amazing color variations and unique personality traits that discus do. Many hobbyists have developed "discus fever" and have quickly formed a lifelong association with this beautiful member of the cichlid family.

Over the years, discus have acquired an unjustified reputation for being difficult to maintain and breed in the home aquarium. But, as with many other types of tropical fish, lack of knowledge concerning a particular aquatic animal's housing requirements has led to quite a bit of misinformation on their care. Once you understand the discus' natural environment, history, water requirements, diet and breeding habits, you'll have the knowledge to successfully keep this species healthy in a home aquarium, and to develop a long relationship with one of the most beautiful and fascinating fish on earth.

Natural Environment

Discus are native to the Colombian, Peruvian, Brazilian and Venezuelan regions of South America. Research has shown that discus seem to live in very close proximity to the Amazon River. Discus tend to reside in family groups that do not stray far from their immediate surroundings. Within these groups, individual discus bear a strong resemblance to each other. A family of discus that is living nearby will be quite different in appearance from their neighbors.

The natural habitat for discus consists of rivers and lakes such as the Urubu River in Brazil, which has slow-moving waters. These native waters tend to be very soft, murky and shallow. Discus are docile and shy, and will spend most of their day lingering beneath large rocks, submerged tree limbs and logs. The cooler temperatures in these shady, sunken areas are a lifesaver during the hottest part of the day.

Collection

Aborigines refer to the discus as "Acara Discu," and it is used extensively as a food staple in their diet. Natives often poison small areas of a river or stream. They do so using timbo (raw rotenone, a substance obtained from the roots of certain tropical plants) and will then gather dead discus and other fish in their nets as they float to the top of the water. Discus are not considered a delicacy by the natives, as their bodies are thin and bony and do not provide much meat.

Collection of discus by local villagers for transport to aquarium hobbyists do not always yield large amounts of surviving specimens. Vast numbers of discus die during the collection and transportation process because of rough handling, poor water conditions, stress and shock. Only a small number of discus survive long enough to become acclimated to dealer and hobbyist tanks.

Wild-caught discus are available to hobbyists, but being trapped and transported is very stressful for the fish.

CAPTURING METHODS

Collection of live discus is not an easy task. Often these fish must be netted one by one as they hide among the tangled tree branches and logs. Villagers and aquatic collectors often jump up and down on top of partially submerged fallen trees and shake them roughly in an attempt to frighten the discus out into the open where they can be easily netted. After dark, villagers will also blind the discus with a bright light and then net them before they are able to escape.

Another common method of catching discus is to encircle a submerged tree with a large net. Next, the villagers will climb into the water and cut up the tree with an ax. The tree limbs are removed from the area, and then the net is drawn in at the center to trap the discus. One of the disadvantages of this capture method is that much of the natural environment is destroyed during the process. Large numbers of discus are often removed during a single net capture. Until the commercial breeding industry began offering discus in large quantities a few years ago, the natural breeding populations were in danger of extinction.

With the help of commercial hatcheries around the world, discus are now being bred in a wide variety of beautiful colors. Fancy new strains have almost eliminated most of the public's demand for the dull brown and pale green varieties found in the Amazon region.

POPULAR DISCUS STRAINS

There are so many beautiful discus from which to choose. Some of the more popular strains include:

- Turquoise discus
- Marlboro Red
- Hi Fin Blue
- Tangerine discus
- Blue Cobalt

History of the Discus Hobby

In 1840, discus were first discovered by a Viennese ichthyologist named Dr. Johann Jacob Heckel. Shortly after its arrival in Europe, the discus became known by the popular name of pompadour fish or brown discus. Heckel shipped the first discus specimens in 55-gallon drums to Germany via a dirigible. Unfortunately, many of his new and rare acquisitions died during transport due to unsuitable shipping conditions and the overall length of their journey.

The discus was introduced into the aquarium hobby in 1933. After the discus made its grand appearance, it slowly began to work its way into the hands of hobbyists who longed to breed this remarkable fish. In 1949, W.T. Dodd began the first successful breeding program of discus in large quantities. Several years later, commercial organizations in Hong Kong, Singapore and Bangkok began breeding discus in large hatcheries to provide numerous species available to the public.

Another pioneer in discus breeding was Danny Dicoco, who successfully hybridized discus fish in many different combinations. From 1956 through 1966, Dicoco supplied the New York market with tank-bred discus. Dr. Eduard Schmidt, a German gynecologist, was another contributor to the new and exciting field of discus breeding. He bred massive quantities of discus to supply other dealers and hobbyists. A few years later while on an expedition, Dr. Herbert Axelrod and Harald Schultz brought back a wild Lake Tefe green discus named *Symphysodon aequifasciata aequifasciata,* which ultimately became the cornerstone for discus breeding in later years.

The blue discus, Symphysodon aequifasciata haraldi, *was first available to hobbyists in the 1960s.*

SUPPLY AND DEMAND

In 1960, other species of discus began to make their appearance in the aquarium hobby. Limited selections of the *Symphysodon aequifasciata aequifasciata* or Green discus, the *Symphysodon aequifasciata haraldi* or Blue discus and the *Symphysodon discus* also known as the Heckel or "native discus" were consistently being made available to the average aquarium hobbyist.

EARLY TRIALS AND ERRORS

When the discus were first introduced into the hobby, many people had difficulty keeping these fish in good health for long periods of time. Hobbyists' efforts to breed their new aquatic pet continually failed simply because they did not have the necessary knowledge to understand their living requirements. But times have changed, and reliable information on discus is now easily obtained.

Years ago, many breeders produced weak strains that were very susceptible to disease. Shipments of diseased fish from other countries were also commonplace, and often illnesses did not manifest until after the discus were placed in the hobbyist's care.

Moreover, many discus died during this early period because the crude collection and inefficient shipping processes of that time caused undue distress for the captured specimens. These roughly treated fish generally had short life spans and were susceptible to disease and bad health. Only through the persistence of hobbyists who wanted to understand the requirements of their new found aquatic friends were lessons learned and mistakes minimized to advance the evolution and art of discus keeping. Hobbyists and breeders quickly learned the secrets of water quality and other environmental requirements that were necessary to keep healthy specimens alive.

In the early years, all discus were captured from their native habitat in the tributary waters of the Amazon and shipped to various locations around the world to be introduced into the retail market. As the years passed, many captive-bred specimens began to flood into the aquarium marketplace. These new variations helped to meet the demand of an ever-growing discus industry. The discus quickly became popular all over

the world. Today, most of the discus that are supplied
to the aquarium industry are captive-bred.

A New Breed

Discus breeding is one of the fastest growing industries
in the aquarium market as we embark upon the new
century. The discus has become
one of the most admired and
respected species of the freshwater aquarium, due to the success
of the breeding facilities that provide an ample supply of beauti-
fully colored discus to fill the
increasing demand. Today there
are so many different varieties
available that it can be very difficult to keep up with all of the new
strains that appear every month.
The first discus were very bland
in appearance. The discus that
you can purchase today are strik-
ing in color, shape and finnage design. Through constant study of the species and experimental selective
breeding, the supply of new and more beautiful discus
seems unending. There is a color to match almost any
hobbyist's individual taste.

*Today, the variety
of captive-bred
discus, such as
this striking
broad-banded
royal, is mind-
boggling.*

Setting the Record Straight

Until the 1990s, many hobbyists believed that the
discus was a poor selection for the home aquarium
because they did not have the confidence to raise that
particular species. While it is true that you can not
guarantee that every fish you buy will remain healthy
and live for a long time, the discus is a relatively safe
bet for any amateur hobbyist who has patiently learned
a few rules concerning its care.

If you provide your discus with an inadequate environment, it will not thrive for long. But this is true of any
other species of tropical fish. Meeting the needs of a
discus is not as hard as many hobbyists think. In fact,

11

Discus may appear unique, but like all tropical fish, they simply need the right environment.

it is a goal that can be easily achieved. Experienced aquarium keepers should not deter any new hobbyist from obtaining, maintaining and breeding the beautiful discus that he longs to have in his own home.

How to Obtain a Discus

Obtaining discus is really very easy. Most pet stores can order these fascinating fish, or you can purchase them from various breeders whom you can find on the Internet. It is important to remember to use caution and be very selective when buying discus. Always choose specimens that look healthy and are being sold by reputable dealers. Investigate a dealer carefully before you purchase any fish from his stock.

The choices that you make in the very beginning are the key factors to your success or failure. If you take the time to thoroughly research all possible avenues pertaining to your individual species, you will be on your way to becoming a successful fish keeper.

THE IMPORTANCE OF A GOOD ENVIRONMENT

In order to appreciate the health and well-being of your discus, you need to remember that your aquarium is going to be their permanent home. If something goes wrong in their native habitat, discus can easily move to a new spot. Unfortunately, they do not have that option in the home aquarium. You must provide proper care, and replace the biological, chemical and mechanical forces of nature that you've removed by placing your pet in a tank.

Keep in mind that you must always strive to imitate your species' natural environment as much as is humanly possible. Creating a natural environment does not mean that you have to replicate the natural setting in exact physical detail; this will simply not be possible. Instead, you should strive to accommodate your discus by providing them with suitable substitutes if natural objects cannot be located through your dealer (such as native logs and rocks).

Setting It All Up

The method that you choose to set up your aquarium will have a strong bearing on how well your fish will thrive. Water chemistry, substrate, lighting, plants and decorations all play important roles in your aquatic pet's well-being. Yes, you could provide a bare bottom tank and filtration, and your discus will probably survive. Or you could furnish your discus aquarium with plants from the Amazon, proper lighting, good nutrition and your discus will flourish with radiant health. When all is said and done, it is still your decision as to what type of environment that you will furnish. Just remember that your aquarium setup will ultimately affect whether your fish happily thrive or simply survive!

> **DON'T FORGET— YOUR FISH TANK IS YOUR FISH'S UNIVERSE**
>
> Never settle for second best as far as aquarium conditions are concerned. Always provide your discus with the best aquarium conditions possible so that it will achieve maximum growth and maintain good health. Your discus will reward you with many years of joy for supplying a natural and stress-free environment.

chapter 2

Discus
Basics
and Behavior

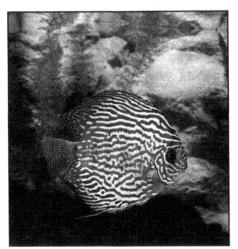

For the beginning hobbyist, the classification of discus may be a little overwhelming at first. But rest assured, it will only take a short time for you to get accustomed to using the different names. Before you know it, you'll sound like an old pro.

Understanding Species

The genus *Symphysodon* is traditionally divided into two different species, *Symphysodon discus* and *Symphysodon aequifasciata*, and five different subspecies. The following table should help you to understand the main discus species classification system, so that you will know exactly what you are buying.

1) Genus: *Symphysodon*
   A) Species: *Symphysodon discus*
      i) Subspecies: *Symphysodon discus discus* (Heckel or Red discus)
      ii) Subspecies: *Symphysodon discus willischwartzi* (Pineapple discus)
2) Genus: *Symphysodon*
   A) Species: *Symphysodon aequifasciata*
      i) Subspecies: *Symphysodon aequifasciata aequifasciata* (Green discus)
      ii) Subspecies: *Symphysodon aequifasciata axelrodi* (Brown discus)
      iii) Subspecies: *Symphysodon aequifasciata haraldi* (Blue discus)

HECKEL DISCUS

The Heckel discus is native to central Brazil. This species carries nine vertical stripes on its side. The first, fifth and ninth stripes are more prominent than the others. The fifth stripe is also thicker than those around it. The first stripe runs right though the eye area; the second, third and fourth in the frontal region; and the fifth through the center of the body. The sixth, seventh and eighth stripes lead up to the ninth, which runs along the base of the caudal (tail) fin.

One of many stunning hybrids is the Red Spotted Green discus.

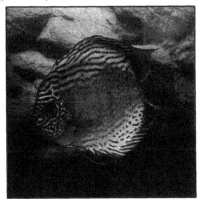

Heckel discus are not as popular as other strains because they are difficult to breed and many hobbyists do not care for the striped look that they carry. Those available are usually caught from the wild. Through crossbreeding, a male Heckel is often bred with a female of another type.

GREEN DISCUS

Most green discus come from Peru. In spite of their name, they tend to have a brownish-green body color.

Brown Discus

The brown discus is usually found at the mouth of the Amazon. It has a brown body with brown or reddish-colored fins.

Blue Discus

The blue discus originate in the Manaus region, and have a brownish-purple body with blue-colored stripes.

Wild Forms and Hybrids

The following chart will describe a few of the more popular wild species and give examples of the wild varieties from which the hybrids were bred. Remember that this chart is only an example of a chosen few, and does not include every different color variation that is now available.

Through selective breeding, the Red Turquoise discus became available to hobbyists.

Color Strains	Wild Forms	Captive-Bred & Hybrids
Blue discus	Blue discus	Striped Turquoise
	Royal Blue discus	Solid Turquoise
		Blue Cobalt
		Blue Diamond
Green discus	Wild Green discus	J.W. Green Mamba
		Rio Japura
		Red Spotted Green
		Lago Coari
Heckel or red discus		Hybrid Red discus
		Pigeon Blood discus
		J.W. Panda discus
		Spotted Marlboro Red
		Red Turquoise discus

Social Skills

A few social factors should be considered when you are purchasing discus for the home aquarium. You want to make absolutely sure that your new aquatic pets get along well with each other and their tankmates.

SOCIALIZING WITH OTHER DISCUS

Discus are not loners by nature, and should be kept with a group of tankmates that are of the same species. A single discus will not be very happy or survive for a long period of time if it is the only fish in the aquarium. Discus prefer to live within a colony of their own kind or similar species. A single specimen in a tank can easily become stressed from sheer loneliness, and may stop eating or become more susceptible to poor health and disease.

Discus have a calm nature, and like to school in groups of at least five or more fish, which will form the basis of their social colony. The size of the colony that you can keep will greatly depend on the size of the tank you are going to use. As a rule, each discus should be given six to ten gallons of water for its own personal space. So, if you want to start with five medium to large discus, you will need at least a 30-gallon tank to keep them from constantly squabbling.

**FIVE SIGNS OF
A COMPATIBLE
DISCUS AQUARIUM**

1. There are no discus hiding in corners to avoid tankmates.

2. One or two discus are not hogging all of the food at feeding time.

3. All of the discus in the aquarium are active and alert.

4. The discus don't display extreme pecking orders and marked territories.

5. The discus don't have torn fins.

OTHER SUITABLE TANKMATES

There are many factors to be taken into consideration when selecting suitable tankmates from other species of fish. Tankmates should not be aggressive, or your discus may end up being chased away from the dinner table and not receive their fair share of the meal. Good tankmates will need to have a calm nature, be somewhat slow-moving, have a docile attitude and be parasite-free.

It is not worth losing hundreds of dollars worth of fish by introducing a species that is known to frequently carry parasites.

Some hobbyists have successfully kept angelfish and discus together. However, there is a risk involved in this cohabitation because some angelfish carry a latent disease such as "cappilaria," which has no ill affect on them but can wipe out an entire colony of discus that are housed in the same tank. Angelfish should be in optimal health before they are added to a discus aquarium.

The most suitable nonspecies tankmates should come from the larger members of the dwarf gourami and rasbora species.

THE SAFEST ARRANGEMENT

To be successful with discus, the safest way to maintain them is to keep them with members of their own species and exclude any other types of fish from their aquarium. There are only a few other species of fish that will thrive in the particular water parameters that discus require. Your discus will also breed more often when they are not disturbed by other species of fish in their tank.

On occasion, aquarists will keep angelfish with their discus, but most people keep discus-only tanks.

Serious breeders don't keep any other types of fish with their discus, and would probably advise you to do the same thing. Why risk losing your investment by adding considerably less expensive species of fish to your show tank that could bring a multitude of diseases or parasites with them and destroy everything that you have worked so hard to accomplish? If you do decide to keep other species with your discus, you will have to carefully quarantine any new additions before adding them to your tank.

Most hobbyists have more than one aquarium setup in their home, which allows them the versatility to own a variety of species without having to keep several different kinds of fish in the same tank. Having more than one aquarium will also provide you with the opportunity to set up species tanks where you can observe how fish naturally interact in the wild. Discus often reveal more natural behavior patterns if they are not kept in a tank with fish that they wouldn't encounter in their native habitat.

Discus aren't elitists, they're just more comfortable with other discus than they are with unfamiliar fish.

Discus Behaviors

Some behaviors are "typical discus" conduct that you should expect to see them exhibit.

LYING ON THEIR SIDE

When transporting your discus, it will often lie on its side in the plastic bag or carrying container. This is normal and is its way of saying, "I'm not happy right now, so I think I'll pout for a while." Some discus will also display this behavior when they are first placed into their new home aquarium. Don't worry, they will get over it soon enough.

AGGRESSIVE BEHAVIOR

Aggression is a problem that usually only manifests during spawning or mating rituals because the breeding couple will feel the need to protect their spawning site from intruders. Discus usually have a limited pecking order that they use to establish dominance within their colony, but it quickly subsides after the boss has been chosen. Young discus often display playful behaviors that are mistaken for aggression. This physical contact between juveniles is similar to young children roughhousing in a schoolyard. It is part of the natural process of learning social behaviors. There are cases where particular strains of discus, such as the Pigeon Blood, are a little bit more aggressive than others.

THE PROBLEM CHILD

Discus are like any other social animal. There are a few bad apples in every group. If you have a particular discus that is terrorizing its tankmates, it's best to offer it to another hobbyist who may have fish that are more compatible with its aggressive nature.

A healthy discus tank will include a lot of activity and good-natured horseplay within the colony. A slow-moving or sluggish group that seems to have little or no reaction to stimuli may be in declining health. Remember, it may take your new discus a few weeks to gain a sense of security in their new aquarium environment, so don't expect boisterous behavior right after you have brought them home from a dealer.

ADJUSTING TO HUMANS

Discus often take quite a while to adjust to their new aquarium surroundings and their human handlers. But when they finally do, they will become as attached to their owners as the family dog. Many discus can be trained to eat right out of your hand and will rush over to the glass everytime you enter into the room. This is simply their way of saying that they are glad to see you.

COLOR CHANGE

Modifications to a discus' physical aquarium environment, such as rearranging the decorations or adding a new piece of driftwood, will often cause them a little stress. In response, the fish will frequently change to a darker color. After a short period of time, they will return to their natural color. Short-term color changes are usually not a sign of ill health. If your discus change to a darker color and then remain that way without returning to their normal hue within a few minutes, it could be a warning sign that they have become diseased or heavily stressed due to a water problem. If this occurs, you should check the water parameters immediately.

SHYNESS

Because your new discus are shy by nature, it's best to keep their aquarium lighting to a minimum. If increased lighting is required because of live aquarium plants, you will need to provide your discus with plenty of hidden retreats (which can be formed from plants, rocks and driftwood) so that they'll have a place to calm their nerves if they become frightened.

Plants and rocks provide your bashful discus a place to hide.

"HUNTING"

Discus seem to enjoy seeking out and capturing live food, particularly during the rainy season, when insects proliferate on the water's surface. The thrill of the chase cannot be eliminated through captive breeding or confinement behind four glass walls. You should periodically provide your fish with live foods so that they can go hunt for a meal. Chasing prey (often with high bursts of speed) is a way that you can get your discus to remain active and "stay in shape."

Setting
Up

part two

the
Discus
Aquarium

chapter 3

The **Aquarium**
and Its
Components

You've probably seen a variety of different aquariums during your lifetime and were captured by the beauty that you found in a discus tank. Discus are freshwater fish, and because a freshwater aquarium is the most practical system for a beginning fish keeper, you've made a wise choice.

A freshwater system is relatively inexpensive to set up, and the fish that live in it are usually easy to obtain. Your discus will be living in a tropical (rather than a cold-water) aquarium. Because your livestock will consist predominantly of discus, you'll be keeping a species tank. A species tank houses fish that come from a similar family. Because freshwater aquariums are the most popular type among hobbyists, you'll have plenty of opportunities to exchange

24

valuable information, equipment, magazines and live-stock with other enthusiasts.

The Natural Environment

It's important to research the type of system that you are interested in so that you will know how to work all of your equipment correctly. Just as important is the research that you will need to do in order to find out as much as your can about your discus' natural environment. When you do, you'll have the knowledge to set up your aquarium correctly. This book will help you with that aspect of setting up your system. I have already given you some information on the Amazon region, but there is always so much more new information to be found! Creating a natural stress-free environment will provide your discus with the best opportunity possible to live long and healthy lives.

Placing Your Aquarium

When deciding where to place your aquarium in your home, you'll need to take your time and choose wisely. There are many household factors that can affect the success of your aquarium system. You'll need to carefully inspect the place that you have initially chosen to set up your aquarium so that you'll be aware of any hazards that may be present.

When choosing a location, consider who else in the home is going to benefit or be upset by the aquarium's placement in a certain area. Are you setting up your discus aquarium as a family project that everyone will enjoy? If that's your goal, you may want to place it in an area where everyone will have the opportunity to look at it without disrupting any family routines. For example, if it were a family aquarium, you would not want to put it in your

> **FIVE TIPS ON AQUARIUM STANDS**
>
> 1. Always place your aquarium stand away from windows and doors.
>
> 2. Periodically inspect your stand for warping or weakness.
>
> 3. Purchase a stand that matches your aquarium size.
>
> 4. Do not place an aquarium on a wobbly stand or poorly made furniture.
>
> 5. Keep your aquarium stand away from high traffic areas.

bedroom. If you want to have your discus in an area that is private, a home office may be a good choice.

Even if you purchase the best equipment that money can buy, your aquarium is still going to make some kind of noise, even if it is only a small gurgle now and then. One person's gurgle may be another's headache. Most people will really enjoy all of the neat little sounds that your tank will make. Unfortunately, there are those who find the noise annoying. If aquarium sounds are going to bother a member of your household, you may want to place your tank in an area that he or she does not frequent often.

Be sure to place your discus tank in a room that is of moderate temperature— your fish won't be happy in a cold basement!

Your aquarium should never be placed in an area that gets extremely hot or very cold. Even if your house is well built and has a lot of insulation, there are undoubtedly areas that receive too much direct sunlight or excessive drafts. Extreme temperature fluctuations of the aquarium water can cause your discus to contract disease.

FINDING A GOOD FIT

Once you've decided which room will be best for your aquarium, you'll need to take a quick measurement of the intended placement space so that you'll know which size tank to buy. You never want to cram an aquarium into a small space because you'll probably have a few pieces of equipment that will hang off the back of the tank. You will need to leave a few extra inches to compensate for filters, hoses and other types of "hot" (hang on tank) equipment.

To clean and maintain your tank, you'll want to leave room to spare in the back so that you can easily reach behind it without putting yourself or your aquarium at risk. If you have to squeeze in behind a tank to clean it, the job will be much more difficult.

If you're wondering how large most tanks really are, the following table will provide you with a few space requirements (length by width by height) of some standard aquarium sizes. Remember to add a few inches on to these figures so that you will have room for equipment and cleaning.

Tank Capacity	Tank Shape	Dimensions
10 Gallon	Regular	20" × 10" × 12"
	Long	24" × 8" × 12"
	Hexagonal	14" × 12" × 18"
20 Gallon	High	24" × 12" × 16"
	Long	30" × 12" × 12"
	Hexagonal	18" × 16" × 20"
30 Gallon	Regular	36" × 12" × 16"
	Breeding	36" × 18" × 12"
40 Gallon	Long	48" × 13" × 16"
	Hexagonal	18" × 16" × 20"
	Breeding	36" × 18" × 16"
55 Gallon	Regular	48" × 13" × 20"
75 Gallon	Regular	48" × 18" × 20"
100 Gallon	Regular	72" × 18" × 18"
125 Gallon	Regular	72" × 18" × 22"
200 Gallon	Regular	84" × 24" × 25"

IRREGULAR TANKS

Odd-shaped aquariums (bubble, hexagon) may look nice, but they do pose challenges. A tank that is tall and thin will have a lesser amount of gas exchange than an aquarium that has a longer and larger surface area. Tanks that are oddly shaped can be more difficult to clean and decorate, and finding equipment to fit an unusually shaped tank can be quite a chore. If you do happen to locate what you're looking for, expect to pay much more for the product.

If you run across an older tank at a local garage sale, it may be hard to estimate the tank's total capacity. Although aquarium tank sizes have become somewhat standardized, many older tanks are not. A good way to obtain total gallonage for a rectangle-shaped aquarium is to multiply the length times the width times the height and then divide that figure by 231.

$$\text{Total Gallons} = \frac{\text{Length} \times \text{Width} \times \text{Height}}{231}$$

WINDOWS AND DOORS

If you place your aquarium near a window, it will receive a lot of direct sunlight. A window's light can cause the water temperature in your tank to reach lethal levels in a very short period of time. Windows also tend to leak air, and these drafts can cause the water to turn cold in the winter. Even the best aquarium heater will have a hard time competing with a winter's draft.

TESTING FOR LEAKS

To test an aquarium for leaks, simply fill it with water and let it stand on a sheet of newspaper in your garage or basement. If the newspaper beneath it is wet after twenty-four hours, then it has a leak. To repair a leak, drain and dry the tank, and then carefully remove the old silicone (only the cracked or peeling parts) with a razor blade. After the old silicone has been cleaned off, replace it with new sealer. Let the new sealer dry for forty-eight hours before you add any water to the tank.

Another major problem that you're going to have with your aquarium if you place it by a window is an excess growth of algae. Algae is good in small amounts because your discus will enjoy picking at it to receive a nourishing treat now and then. But when algae growth gets out of control, you're going to have a hard time getting rid of it.

Any door that leads to the outside of your home can be very drafty and will allow cold air in during the winter months. It doesn't take long for an aquarium to chill under these adverse conditions. Make sure that you place you tank well away from any doors that lead outside. Inside doors can damage your aquarium if they are accidentally pushed into it. Check for clearance by opening and closing any door that is in close proximity to the area where you want to place your tank. A few minutes of testing will help you avoid an expensive disaster.

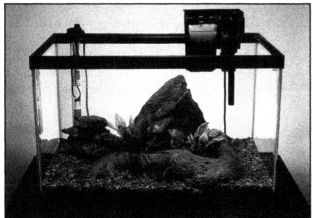

Find a relatively peaceful spot for your tank. Too much activity will aggravate your discus.

HIGH TRAFFIC AREAS

Hallways, dining rooms and kitchens are not good areas for aquarium placement. If people are continually moving back and forth past the tank, your discus may become stressed out. High traffic areas also increase the risk of the aquarium being knocked over or broken. If you have small children in your home, they need to be taught to respect the aquarium and the fish that live in it. Childproof your aquarium chemicals by locking them up in a separate location.

WATER SUPPLY

The area where your aquarium is going to stand should have an available water outlet. You don't want to be forced to carry a bunch of heavy buckets of water around in order to do water changes. Even a hose can become cumbersome if the water outlet is too far away. You will have to have water to fill up your tank when you first set it up, and you will also to need to periodically add water to replace levels lost to evaporation.

POWER OUTLETS

Don't make the mistake of finding a prime location for your aquarium, only to realize a short while later that there is no electrical outlet close by. All outlets near the

aquarium should be in good working order. You may have to use a multiplug extension depending on the total number of plug-ins that your equipment has. Make sure that any extensions you use have a surge protector built in.

Financial Considerations

Your aquarium tank will probably be the largest investment that you'll encounter in your new hobby. But don't forget that items such as gravel, nets, air hose, fil-

A large rectangular tank is best for your discus. The surface-to-air ratio of the tank is much larger than that of a bowl.

ters, pumps, chemicals, airstones and heaters should be taken into consideration when you are calculating your budget for your complete system. You will also need to add in the price of your discus as well. But don't worry, it will all be worth it when you find yourself relaxing in front of your new discus tank after a hard day's work.

Starter Kits

Starter kits are relatively inexpensive and come packaged in a single box. A basic kit usually offers a 10-, 20- or 40-gallon tank along with a hood, filter, thermometer, net, heater, fish food, water conditioner and a small instructional book. As a rule, decorations and gravel must be purchased separately.

For a discus tank, you'll need to purchase an aquarium that is at least thirty gallons. Anything smaller is going to make your fish very uncomfortable. A larger tank will provide a better surface for gas exchange (carbon dioxide for oxygen). Smaller tanks are not very stable, and can become lethal should a power or heater failure occur. You should always buy the largest tank that your financial budget and space limitations will allow.

Places to Buy Aquariums and Equipment

Local pet supply shops are a good place to begin your shopping. Dealer's tanks usually have a warranty and are generally in good condition. If you do happen to have any problems with your tank or equipment, you can usually return them for a refund. A dealer can also help you choose the right system for your discus, and give you a few pointers on other aspects of the hobby.

SUPERSTORES

Most superstores (which sell clothing, pets, hardware and the like) carry aquarium tanks and equipment, but you'll usually not find a wide selection of products. Employees in these types of stores are often trained in the basic essentials of aquarium keeping but do not have the aquatic knowledge to deal with higher level problems. It is also very rare to find a discus at a superstore. The aquatic livestock carried in many superstores are unlikely to receive the level of care that a pet dealer will provide.

Your discus will thrive if you keep its needs in mind when setting up its home.

GARAGE SALES

Hobbyists can get a great deal on aquarium tanks and equipment at a garage sale, but they will not come with a guarantee. If you purchase a used tank at a garage sale, you will need to carefully inspect it for leaks, cracks and worn silicone. Make sure that the silicone seal (the clear rubber-like substance in the seams) is not peeling, cracked (or missing altogether!). Also be aware that used equipment can pose an electrical hazard if it has worn parts or frayed cords.

BUILDING YOUR OWN

Unless you really know how to work with glass, you shouldn't attempt to build your own aquarium. Glass cutting can be dangerous and is better off left in the hands of experts. It's much safer to purchase a tank at a dealer than risk building an inferior product that may leak or have serious pressure problems.

Moving an Aquarium

Never try to move an aquarium by yourself. Aquariums are very heavy, and trying to lift one on your own is a good way to damage your back. When you're ready to move your tank, find a couple of friends to help you out. Make sure that all decorations have been removed and that the aquarium has been completely drained of all water before you attempt to lift it. Do not grab the top of the frame and use it as a makeshift handle to lift the tank. Lifting an aquarium by its frame can damage the sealer and glass. The best way to lift an aquarium is to have everyone place their hands beneath the bottom corners of the tank and then lift the unit evenly.

chapter 4

Understanding
Equipment

The Aquarium Tank

There are three basic types of aquarium tanks that you can buy for your discus system: plastic, glass and acrylic. Each type of tank has its own advantages and disadvantages. The final decision on a tank's purchase will usually involve personal taste and available finances.

GLASS TANKS

Glass aquariums are by far the most popular of all tanks, and are readily available at almost any pet supply store. They are tightly sealed with silicone and do not scratch easily. Glass aquariums can be tempered (stronger and light-weight) or plate (heavier and thicker). They will also provide you with a proper viewing area because all of the walls on the aquarium are completely flat.

Glass aquariums have a few disadvantages. If you want a really modern-looking tank with an unusual shape, you won't find much variety with glass tanks because they can only be molded into a limited number of shapes. Glass aquariums are very heavy, especially when they are larger than twenty gallons. If you have weak floors in your home, you may be limited to pur-chasing smaller-sized tanks.

ACRYLIC

Acrylic tanks are lightweight and are available in a vast array of shapes and sizes. Common styles include con-vex, concave, bubble, tube and triangular. An acrylic tank will have a minute amount of distortion because the material is bent during construction of the aquar-ium. Acrylic tanks have a seamless look in the corners allowing for uninterrupted viewing.

Acrylic tanks have a very eye-pleasing look that has not yet been replicated in a standard glass aquarium. Because they are lighter than glass, an acrylic aquar-ium will allow you to have a much larger tank in an area that can only support a limited amount of weight. Many acrylic aquariums are manufactured with col-ored backgrounds, which can be quite beautiful. Acrylic is also much stronger than glass, and blemishes can be removed from the surface with a simple scratch remover kit.

PLASTIC TANKS

Plastic tanks are very inexpensive, but they have seri-ous disadvantages. Problems with plastic tanks are that they turn yellow with age, have a distorted view, scratch easily and cannot be fixed if they crack. Plastic tanks are generally available only in very small sizes (usually between two and six gallons) and do not have enough surface area or volume to provide stability for a discus community.

The Stand

An aquarium stand should be constructed of a solid material. To prevent buckling, the stand should be able to hold at least 100 pounds more than the total weight of your aquarium system. It is not a good idea to use household furniture as an aquarium stand because it may eventually warp or have its finish ruined by water leaks or evaporation dribbles. An aquarium should always fit a stand correctly. Do not allow the tank to hang over the sides.

The aquarium stand should be placed on a solid surface. Any movement of the floor beneath the aquarium may cause the tank to break. If you're living in a mobile home, upstairs apartment or older home, you should carefully inspect the floor and supports to make sure that they will be able to withstand the increased pressure.

Your discus won't weigh much, but the tank is really heavy. Be certain that the stand can support the tank and that your floor is nice and solid!

CABINET STANDS

Cabinet stands are enclosed on the bottom so that you'll be able to hide equipment that might detract from the beauty of your aquarium system. Medicines, nets, chemicals, filters, pumps and test kits can be conveniently stored behind the cabinet's doors. Cabinet stands can be expensive but are worth the extra investment. These stands can be special-ordered to fit almost any size aquarium tank.

WROUGHT IRON STANDS

Wrought iron stands are made of thin metal. The underside of the stand is open and often comes with a single shelf for supporting pumps and other types of equipment. Wrought iron stands are less expensive than cabinets but will not provide you with the opportunity to hide your equipment from plain view.

TOTAL WEIGHT

Remember that a 55-gallon tank will weigh close to 550 pounds when it is completely set up. To estimate any aquarium weight, simply multiply the total number of gallons by 10. The stand must be able to support the weight comfortably.

Filtration Systems

Filters play a very important role in the biological, mechanical and chemical functions of your aquarium system. All three are required for your discus to remain healthy. Filtration promotes the nitrogen cycle, so that essential bacteria can thrive to break down wastes in your system. Filtration also removes wastes through chemical reactions and by mechanically removing it from the water. A good filter will also help to aerate the water. Some types of filters provide only one function; others may be able to accomplish two, or all three.

MECHANICAL FILTRATION

Mechanical filtration removes solid wastes and debris that are suspended in the water. This process is accomplished when aquarium water is trapped in a filter's medium. Common mediums for mechanical filtration include foam and floss that are usually stored in a cartridge or slot within the filter. After a short period of time, bacteria will grow on the filter's medium, and it will begin to play a role in the biological cycle as well.

BIOLOGICAL FILTRATION

Biological filtration occurs when bacteria colonies begin to thrive on a filter's surface (usually in the medium or beneath a filter plate) to convert deadly ammonia (produced by fish waste) and food debris into less harmful substances known as nitrites and nitrates. The larger the surface area on the filter's medium, the more nitrifying bacteria your cycle will have. Media can be thrown away, rinsed or reused depending on your particular filter.

CHEMICAL FILTRATION

Chemical filtration relies on the adsorption of molecular compounds in the filter media to clean impurities from the aquarium's water. Activated mediums, such as zeolite and charcoal, absorb chemicals and dissolve minerals when aquarium water is passed over them.

Filters

There are many different types of filters to choose from. It's always best to have at least two different filters on your system, just in case one fails. The combination of the two filters should produce mechanical, biological and chemical filtration.

SPONGE FILTER

A sponge filter is often used for biological filtration in a hospital or fry tank because it will not destroy medications or suck small fry up into its unit. This type of filter is attached to an air pump. The pump draws aquarium water though a large sponge that provides an area for bacteria colonization.

UNDERGRAVEL FILTER

Undergravel filters are one of the best systems to use when you start your discus aquarium. Undergravel filters provide biological filtration. If you add a mechanical filter to your aquarium (such as a power filter), you'll have all of the essentials covered.

An undergravel filter pulls water down through the gravel so that bacteria (that live in the space beneath) can break down waste as it passes beneath the plate. The water is then returned to the aquarium through the uplift tubes. Debris is also trapped along the substrate bed during this process and can be periodically removed by an aquarium vacuum. A medium-size substrate should be used with an undergravel filter to avoid clogging the plates. An undergravel filter should be set in place before the substrate is added.

Powerheads

Powerheads can be inserted into the top of the uplift tubes on an undergravel filter system. Powerheads are electrically driven units that will increase the filter's output and efficiency by drawing water up through the tubes at a faster rate than a standard air pump.

POWER FILTERS

A power filter is run by an internal motor and hangs on the back of the aquarium. Power filters are usually shaped like a long box and are available in a wide variety of sizes. These types of filters have slots that hold removable floss pads, which contain charcoal. A power filter sucks up tank water through an intake tube, passes it over the pads and then returns it to the aquarium. In time, the pads will build up a bacteria colony, which will perform the biological function of waste reduction.

EQUIPMENT TIPS

1. Purchase the best quality equipment that your finances will allow.

2. Periodically inspect your equipment for worn parts.

3. Never attempt to modify equipment away from its original purpose.

4. Keep all equipment instructions for ordering parts and functional information.

5. Replace worn or damaged equipment immediately.

Bio-Wheel

Some power filters contain a wheel that rotates at the water's surface so that the wheel continually comes in contact with both the air and water. This type of unit is known as a bio-wheel, and it will keep the bacteria colony alive even if you have to change the internal pad.

CANISTER FILTERS

A canister filter is often used on larger aquarium systems. A canister filter contains several compartments that hold a variety of different mediums that carry out the processes of mechanical, chemical and biological filtration. The aquarium water is drawn though these mediums via hoses that are attached to a high-pressure pump, and many units are capable of circulating several hundred gallons per hour. Most canister filters sit on the floor, but a few styles can be hung from the back of the tank.

FLUIDIZED BED FILTERS

A fluidized bed filter uses a column of sand as a biological medium. These filters can be very expensive, but are well worth the money. This filter is used for biological filtration only, so you must also have some other type of mechanical and chemical filters on the aquarium to supplement it.

Heaters

There are two types of heaters that you can purchase for your discus tank. Submersible heaters are placed beneath the water line. This type of unit has a glass tube with a ceramic core, which is completely sealed for safety. Submersible heaters have internal thermostats that allow you to set the temperature to a specific level. A small light indicates when the heater is on. Nonsubmersible heaters hang on the aquarium frame, and the adjustment valve remains above the waterline when you place it on the tank. Temperature adjustments are made in small increments by turning the valve and then checking the temperature repeatedly.

If possible, you should have two heaters operating at the same time should one unit fail. The backup heater will keep the water temperature from dropping until you have time to repair or replace the other. One way to estimate which size heater your aquarium will need is to allow 5 watts per gallon. For example, a 55-gallon aquarium would need a heater that is at least 275 watts.

The glass on a heater can get very hot, even though it's in water. Never plug in a heater until it has adjusted to the aquarium's water temperature. After you place the heater on the tank, wait at least twenty minutes before you plug it in. If you are removing a heater from an older setup, unplug the heater and allow it to remain in the water for twenty minutes before you remove it. Failure to follow these simple rules can result in your heater's glass shattering, cracking or exploding.

Thermometers

Aquarium thermometers are available in several different styles and include units that hang on the tank frame, float in the water or stick to the glass. Severe temperature fluctuations can cause sickness or death, so make sure that you check your thermometer's reading frequently.

Air Pumps

An air pump can be used to power airstones, filters and bubble disks. Aquarium pumps use either a vibrator or piston to produce air. Vibrator pumps are not as expensive as piston pumps and are easy to care for. A poor quality vibrator pump, however, can make a lot of noise. Piston pumps are much more powerful than vibrator pumps, but they do require a little more maintenance. An air pump should be placed above the midpoint level of the aquarium to avoid backflow of water if electrical power is lost. You can do this using a tank or wall mount.

Regardless of the style you choose, make sure that your aquarium thermometer is accurate.

AIRLINE TUBING

Airline tubing is used to connect equipment that is powered by an air pump. You should always have a good supply on hand. Modern silicone/rubber-based tubing is quite flexible and has a natural blue tint that blends in nicely with the aquarium water. The clear tubing originally designed for aquarium use is semirigid and tends to get stiff, crack, kink and yellow with age.

An airstone is used to split up the air that is supplied by the pump into small bubbles. Airstones are usually shaped like a cylinder or block and are constructed of wood or ceramic materials. Short, wide airstones emit a larger stream of bubbles than small ones. Airstones are attached to a pump by airline tubing.

DISKS AND WANDS

If you want to create a larger stream of bubbles, you can always try a bubble disk or wand. A bubble disk is shaped like a dinner plate and puts out a massive amount of bubbles when hooked to a large pump. A bubble wand usually comes with suction cups and is placed along the rear glass to create a stream effect. Bubble wands tend to break easily and become clogged with algae.

Air Valves

An air valve is constructed to hang on the back of the tank, and is usually made out of brass, copper or plastic. To use the valve, hook up one end with tubing that is attached to an aquarium pump. The multiple outlets are then attached to equipment and decorations in the same manner. The strength of the airflow coming out of the valve can be individually adjusted for each piece of equipment or decoration by rotating the shutoff nozzles.

> ### SAFETY FIRST
>
> Small children love to play with aquarium equipment. Make sure that all cords and equipment are out of their reach. Never allow a child to play near an aquarium without adult supervision.

Hoods

A full hood will have a built-in light, and will completely cover the top of your aquarium. Make sure that the hood you purchase fits the tank correctly to prevent water loss from evaporation. An aquarium hood will also help to keep dust and debris from entering the aquarium, protect against heat loss and stop your fish from jumping out of the tank. The plastic canopy beneath the hood will have sections or slots that can be cut out to make room for equipment.

Strip Lights

Strip lights are single units that either rest on top of a glass cover or hang from the ceiling. Strip lights will allow you to add more lighting later on or move the units around.

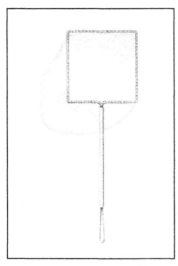

A fishnet is a necessity. You'll probably want to have a few nets of varying sizes.

Other Equipment

Algae Scraper

A scraper is used to remove excess algae from the aquarium glass. Most scrapers have a sponge and bristle pad, which is attached to a long plastic handle. You should clean any unsightly algae off your glass at least once a week.

Fishnets

After you've been in the aquarium hobby for a few months, you'll quickly see that fishnets are a very important commodity to have on hand. Purchase a small selection of different sized nets so that you will always be prepared if you need to move your discus or its tankmates from one aquarium to another.

Aquarium Claws

Aquarium claws have a long handle with a pair of plastic claspers at the end. This tool can be used to pick up objects in the aquarium, such as small rocks and plants, without getting your arms wet.

Buckets

Plastic buckets can be used to make water changes and temporarily hold your fish while your are transporting them to another aquarium.

AQUARIUM SEALER

A tube of silicone aquarium sealer should always be
kept on hand just in case one of your aquariums begins
to leak.

CHEMICALS

Keep a small supply of important chemicals such as
dechlorinator so that you'll always be prepared to
make water changes. Also, a few commercial medications such as ich and fungus formulas should be readily available if your discus become ill.

Setting Up Your Aquarium

Although the steps involved in putting an aquarium
system together may vary slightly depending on which
type of equipment you choose, the following list will
give you a good example of
a complete setup that will
get you started.

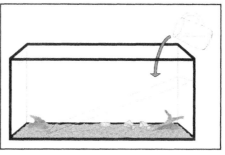

1. Place your stand in the
   proper location.
2. Clean your aquarium
   tank with clear water.
3. Place the tank on the
   stand.

*To keep your
decor intact,
add your water
by pouring it in
over a slanted
surface.*

4. Place the undergravel filter in the aquarium.
5. Add the airline tubing and airstones to the inside
   of the undergravel filter's uplift tubes, and connect them to the aquarium pump.
6. Rinse the gravel in a bucket with clear water.
7. Slowly place the gravel on top of the undergravel
   filter.
8. Arrange the gravel so that it slopes uphill toward
   the rear of the tank.
9. Place your heater in the aquarium.
10. Arrange large decorations such as rocks and drift-
    wood along the bottom.
11. Place any plastic plants that you are using in the
    gravel.

12. Add a power filter to the back of the tank.
13. Fill the aquarium with water.
14. Add dechlorinator to the aquarium's water.
15. Wait twenty minutes, and then plug in the heater, air pump and power filter.
16. Make sure that all of the equipment is functioning properly.
17. Add a thermometer to the tank, and check the water temperature. Adjust the heater if necessary.
18. Check the water's pH and adjust as needed.
19. Place the hood or canopy and lights on top of the aquarium.
20. Plug the lights in.
21. Allow the tank to run for at least twenty-four hours.
22. Recheck the temperature and pH.
23. Add your starter fish (not discus at this point).
24. Sit back and enjoy!

chapter 5

Aquarium
Water

Water is obviously the essence of your discus' environment. If not monitored properly, foul water and poor conditions can cause major health problems. In order to condition and keep your water at the proper temperature, pH and hardness, you'll need to learn a few simple rules and practice some simple procedures. But fear not, maintaining proper water conditions is not as difficult as it may first seem.

Testing and Conditioning Your Water

Before you fill your aquarium for the first time, you should initially test your water to determine the natural chloramine and chlorine,

45

temperature and pH levels. After initial testing is complete, you can then decide on the proper adjustments that you'll need to make in order to meet your fishs' requirements.

WHAT'S IN YOUR WATER?

Chlorine and chloramine are routinely added to the water supply in many parts of the world to eliminate or control bacteria in the drinking water. These two chemicals are usually present in city water and are harmless for human consumption, but they're known to be very toxic to aquarium fish.

The removal of chlorine and chloramine is the first part of the water conditioning process. The safest way to know whether your water contains these two chemicals is to call your local water district and ask if they are used to treat your water supply.

You can add bottled dechlorinator directly to the water to remove the chlorine or chloramine. Make sure that the product you choose is capable of removing both toxins, as some are not effective against chloramine.

The second way that you can safely remove chlorine and chloramine is by allowing your tap water to sit in an open container for at least twenty-four hours prior to adding it into your tank. Place an airstone in the container, and the bubbling action will naturally eliminate the chlorine from the water without the use of any chemicals.

The Nitrogen Cycle

Often, new hobbyists will fill their tanks with water, add a few chemicals and then dump a truckload of fish into the tank all in one day. A week later, they wonder why all of their fish are dying off like flies. The problem is known as "new tank syndrome." Essentially, the aquarium water was poisoned because the bacteria that were needed to eliminate ammonia and nitrites were not present in adequate amounts. In order for a bacterial colony to build, the nitrogen cycle must be allowed to run its full course. This process takes time and patience.

HELPFUL BACTERIA

Within the aquarium environment, beneficial bacteria known as nitrosomonas develop a colony on the filter media and in the substrate to break down the toxic ammonia that is produced by the decomposition of fish waste and other organic matters such as uneaten fish food. The bacteria convert the ammonia into a less toxic substance known as nitrite. However, most fish cannot tolerate high levels of this toxin and will usually begin to show signs of stress immediately after nitrite levels begin to rise. Another type of bacteria known as nitrobacter will then convert the increasingly potent nitrites into nitrates. This entire process is known as the nitrogen cycle.

Nitrates are the end product of the nitrogen cycle, and are harmful when their levels begin to rise. Nitrates can be removed from the aquarium water by performing routine water changes. The entire nitrogen cycle can take quite a while to run its course (usually four to eight weeks) and can be monitored by testing your water frequently with ammonia, nitrite and nitrate test kits. The nitrogen cycle will not begin its process until the first fish has been placed in the tank.

The Nitrogen Cycle

Fish wastes

Food

Decomposers (fungi and bacteria)

Plant fragments and uneaten food

AEROBIC CONDITIONS

Ammonia

Nitrates

Nitrite bacteria

Nitrate bacteria

Nitrates (NO$_2$⁻)

No aeration or filter turned off

Denitrification by anaerobic bacteria
ANAEROBIC CONDITIONS

The nitrogen cycle.

WATCH THE CYCLE UNFOLD

While monitoring the nitrogen cycle with test kits, you'll probably notice that the pH may decrease a little during the conditioning process. This is perfectly normal. But you cannot allow the pH to reduce for long periods of time during cycling because it will prevent beneficial bacteria from multiplying to their full potential. Routine water changes will help to keep the pH, nitrites and nitrates at safe levels while the bacteria multiply.

Chemicals and medications should not be used during the conditioning process because they can impede proper bacterial growth, in turn impeding proper completion of the nitrogen cycle. During the cycling period, you may notice that the water appears cloudy. The cloudiness is a beneficial bacterial bloom, which is a part of the normal cycle. If your aquarium has a proper filtration system, the water should become clear again within a few days.

STARTER FISH

Starter fish such as the zebra danio and guppy are often used to cycle a tank due to their economical price tags and their ability to thrive under poor water

conditions. The nitrogen cycle requires ammonia from fish waste in order to begin its process. Two to four starter fish (per twenty gallons) are generally used to get the ball rolling. When your tank has completed the nitrogen cycle, you can remove the fish

You may want to start your tank with some less expensive fish, such as guppies, before you add your discus.

you used to cycle the tank and either place them in another tank or give them to a friend who has an aquarium system that will suit their needs.

Even though your starter fish will help to begin the process of proper bacterial growth, you must remember that the nitrogen cycle takes time to build up a well-established biological colony. *Don't add too many fish right away* because it will overload the biological filtration system and result in new tank syndrome. Wait until the cycle is complete, and then you can add a few discus to the aquarium each week after removing your starter fish. A *gradual* increase in livestock will keep any additional ammonia levels within a minimum range.

SEEDING AN AQUARIUM

There are also ways to cycle a tank without the use of starter fish. You can seed a filter by placing it on an existing tank and allowing it to become colonized with beneficial bacteria for several weeks. Place the colonized filter onto your new tank, and you'll have a head start on a bacterial colony. In most cases, a small number of fish can be introduced to the tank immediately when a seeded filter is used. Obviously, you must have an established aquarium (or access to a friend's) in order to seed the filter.

PRECOLONIZED MEDIA

Precolonized media products contain live bacteria that can jump-start your biological filter, and in most cases shorten the time it takes to cycle the tank. The media can be directly added to your filter or placed in bags beneath a water flow.

WHEN IS THE CYCLE COMPLETE?

After you've monitored your water and noticed that ammonia has peaked and is beginning to drop off, then phase one of the nitrogen cycle will be complete. After the ammonia levels drop, the nitrite levels will rise and fall. By that time, phase two will be finished. Finally, the nitrate levels will level off, and the cycle will be complete.

Water Hardness

The degree of hardness (dH) is a measurement of the amount of dissolved mineral salts in your water supply. The dH scale runs from 0 (very soft) to 30+ (very hard). Water collects minerals as it travels through the rocks and the earth's soil. These minerals, particularly calcium and magnesium, generate a condition that is commonly referred to as "hardness" or "hard water."

Many hobbyists disagree on the proper dH for discus. However, for normal discus keeping, a medium to slightly hard level (10 to 15 dH), is generally considered acceptable. Higher levels of hardness are known to aid in the growth process of younger discus by providing them with necessary minerals. Lower levels of hardness are known to be more acceptable for breeding situations (3 to 10 dH). Softer water levels tend to make it easier for the female to become impregnated and lay her eggs. Softer water also aids in the egg hatching process.

Although there is disagreement about the correct water hardness for discus, a range of 10 to 15 dH should be suitable.

WATER SOFTENING PROCEDURES

Softening pillows can be purchased at any pet supply shop, and are one of the easiest and most economical ways to soften your water. The little pillows are added to your filtration equipment and are then recharged periodically by soaking them in a saltwater solution. The saltwater solution recharges the resins in the pillow, which allows the pillow to be reused several times before it needs to be replaced.

REVERSE OSMOSIS

A reverse osmosis unit contains a membrane that acts as a molecular filter to remove up to 99 percent of all the dissolved minerals, particles and organic materials larger than a 300 molecular weight. To reverse the process of osmosis, a pump is used to pressurize the feed water flow to the membrane in the unit. The membrane allows the pure water to flow through it while rejecting the passage of any impurities contained in the feed supply. To limit the buildup of impurities on the reverse osmosis membrane, draining washes out a portion of the feed water containing the rejected impurities.

There are a few drawbacks to using the reverse osmosis process. During the process, the water is stripped of any trace elements that are beneficial to the aquarium fish and will have to be replaced by bottled solutions. Often, a fluctuation in the pH level of the water can occur while using this type of unit. Reverse osmosis units can also be very expensive.

USING PEAT MOSS

Peat moss has been used over the years in order to reproduce the natural black water environment found in the Amazon. These same effects can be achieved through the use of black water extracts that are readily available on the market. A bag of peat can be incorporated into the tank's filter system by placing it in an area that will not impede the water flow. Make sure that the area you choose does not allow the peat to be washed out into the aquarium.

Peat releases such items as tannic and humic acids into the water that reduce the pH level and perform as a natural ion exchanger to reduce carbonate hardness. This entire process will create a softening effect. The active compounds in peat are also present in the natural black waters of the Amazon and can aid in controlling heavy metals and other toxins that may be present.

Adding peat to your filtration system will help to reproduce the water quality found in the discus' native habitat.

When using peat in the filtration equipment, you'll notice that it will often color the tank water yellow. This change in water color should not cause any alarm because it is a natural by-product of the tannins and acids leaching out into the water. These tannins will produce a more stress-free and softer environment that discus love. Tannic acids also tend to possess a medical quality that aids in the healing of minor scrapes and scratches, which are common in aquarium fish. Aged peat moss from another aquarium system will soften the water more slowly than new moss.

BOILING

Boiling water, which causes the bicarbonates to break apart and precipitate, can reduce water hardness.

RAINWATER

Another way to soften water is by diluting it with rainwater. Rainwater is soft because it has not picked up any minerals from contact with the earth. Any rainwater you use should be filtered through carbon to remove pollutants before adding it to the tank.

pH

The pH scale that you're going to work with in your aquarium system ranges from 0 to 14. The number 0 is the lowest value on the scale and represents the highest acidic level. The acid scale (which you will use for your discus) runs from 0 to 6.9. The number 14 is the highest value on the scale and represents the highest level of alkalinity (also known as basic). The alkaline scale (which is used for marine systems) runs from 14 down to 7.1. A pH of 7 is considered neutral. Discus prefer a pH that falls between 6.5 and 6.8.

> **AQUATIC TIP**
>
> An extra airstone or bubble disk placed in the back of the aquarium will help to create a more oxygen-enriched atmosphere and will provide a steady current that will keep cold pockets to a minimum.

When you're adjusting your pH level in the tank, take your time and do it in small increments. The best way to change the pH level in your tank is by performing water changes instead of adding any chemicals directly to the aquarium water. Never lower your pH level over two tenths of a point (.2) within a twenty-four-hour period. pH is based on a mathematical logarithmic scale, so a pH of 7 is 10 times more alkaline than a pH of 6, and a pH of 8 is 100 times more alkaline than a pH of 6.

Probably the best plan is to start with a neutral pH (7), and then slowly adjust your level into the acid range. If you have a very high pH level in your tap water, you may want to consider using distilled water instead of your regular tap supply.

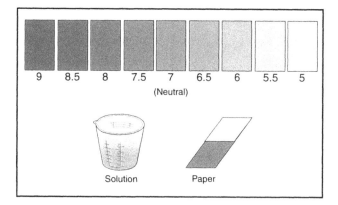

Determining the pH of your aquarium water can be done with simple test kits found at pet supply stores.

Oxygen

It is important to keep a high oxygen level in the discus aquarium. Lower oxygen levels can cause stress, invite disease and stunt normal growth patterns. To keep oxygen levels at a maximum, make sure that your filtration system is working properly.

Water Temperature

Rapid fluctuations in water temperature can be devastating to your discus. Water that is used for water changes should be the same temperature and pH as the main discus tank. For discus fry or young juveniles, temperatures between 85° to 86°F are acceptable. Adult discus can comfortably live in slightly lower temperatures, from 76° to 84°F. Because of their natural tropical habitat, discus are capable of living in water as warm as 90°F with little stress. As water temperature increases, the oxygen concentration decreases, so it's best to use a temperature range within the low 80's and save the higher temperatures for treating disease, breeding and hatching eggs.

HEATERS

To maintain tropical water temperatures within your aquarium environment you should equip your system with reliable heaters. You should always use two heaters in your aquarium, just in case one burns out. The second unit will maintain the tank's temperature if you need to replace the other. A heater should supply 2 watts per gallon. So, a 55-gallon aquarium would need at least a 110-watt heater.

Water Changes

Water changes can help to reduce disease, replenish lost trace elements and provide your discus with good health and maximum growth conditions. One theory holds that adult discus release a growth-inhibiting hormone, which can stunt the growth of a juvenile discus when they are kept together in the same tank. Even though there is no scientific proof available to support this idea, the possibility shouldn't be overlooked. Water changes can reduce that risk.

THE CORRECT WAY TO CHANGE AQUARIUM WATER

1. Remove 20 to 25 percent of the water from the tank after vacuuming the gravel.

2. Clean the inside walls of the aquarium with a clean sponge to remove algae buildup.

3. Prepare new water and make needed adjustments before adding it to the tank.

4. Allow the new water to settle from adjustments that were made.

5. Slowly add the new water to the aquarium and replace the volume that was removed.

IMPORTANCE OF PERFORMING WATER CHANGES

Water changes remove uneaten food and fish waste that accumulate on the tank floor, and supply your aquarium with a constant source of fresh water. The frequency and the amount changed will greatly depend on how many discus you have in you tank. For example, a 55-gallon tank that contains larger discus would certainly require more frequent water changes than if it were lightly populated with smaller fish. Larger numbers of fish in an aquarium will increase the overall biological load.

Two other factors that play an important role in determining the frequency of water changes are the efficiency of the filter system and the feeding schedule. An aquarium with a poor filtration system will require more frequent water changes. Uneaten food that is allowed to accumulate due to overfeeding can foul your tank. If you consistently overfeed your fish, more frequent water changes will be needed.

SCHEDULING YOUR WATER CHANGES

The frequency of water changes is more or less a personal preference and tends to vary a great deal among hobbyists. Some fish keepers perform daily water changes because their schedules allow it. Others change their water weekly or biweekly. Changing 25 percent of the water in a discus tank weekly will keep your aquarium clean. Daily changes can become routine and time-consuming, and are not really necessary. Moreover, if you have to condition your water with the use of chemicals and pH buffers, daily water changes can be cost-prohibitive.

Ultraviolet Sterilization Units

Ultraviolet (UV) sterilization units kill harmful bacteria, microorganisms, free-floating parasites, viruses and fungi that are commonly found in the aquarium water. The water is moved past an ultraviolet light that destroys the parasites. The main advantage of

An ultraviolet sterilization unit destroys parasites, keeping your discus in good health.

using an ultraviolet unit is that if your fish become stressed, the chances of them becoming infected with any waterborne parasites would be greatly reduced. Unfortunately, ultraviolet units can be expensive.

UV MAINTENANCE AND MEDICATING

The lamp inside of the ultraviolet unit usually loses much of its strength in about six to eight months time, and must be replaced in order to keep it functioning properly. If you use an ultraviolet sterilizer, you must turn it off to medicate the aquarium in the event of illness. If the unit is turned back on during the disease treatment, medications that are still present in the water may be broken down into lethal toxins. When you're through medicating the tank, do several water changes before returning your UV unit to its normal service.

Putting It All Together

If you faithfully keep an eye on the water in your aquarium system, your discus will live long and happy lives. Do not allow water conditions to deteriorate. Once water begins to foul, many unpleasant organisms will begin to take over. Always keep ahead of the game by using your test kits to monitor conditions, and by changing water frequently. Your discus will be much happier if you do.

chapter 6

Plants,
Substrate and
Accessories

One of the most beautiful and interesting sights that can be found in a freshwater aquarium is a group of live plants swaying gently in the tank's current. Live plants provide the essence and elegance of nature in its most simplistic form. Why should a hobbyist maintain a bare aquarium, when a healthy group of live plants can provide the fish with a sense of security and bring a serene mood to the aquatic scenery?

In the freshwater aquarium environment, live tropical plants serve many purposes. Live plants release oxygen into the water and the substrate, which is beneficial for aquatic pets, aids in the nitrogen cycle and prevents waste buildup by acting as a natural filtration system. Plants remove organic waste materials that are continually produced within the aquarium system. Dense aquarium plants can also be used to provide shade, protect your water against excess algae and provide good hiding and spawning places for your discus and other aquarium fish. Live plants do not really require a lot of special care, and are well worth investigating in further detail.

Native Plants

Discus really do not require live plants in order to thrive within their aquarium environment because few flora species are found in their natural habitat. But research has shown that discus seem to do well in a planted tank because it provides them with an extra feeling of security. In the wild, the Amazon region contains masses of dead tree roots that have become partially submerged over a sandy silt-covered bottom. An aquarium that has an Amazonian scheme combined with a few live plants can make an interesting and beautiful home for your discus.

FIVE TIPS FOR HEALTHIER PLANTS

1. Select plants that will match your water conditions.

2. Offer consistent lighting that provides a complete spectrum.

3. Periodically feed your plants with aquatic flora fertilizers.

4. Prune dead leaves and stems off of your plants on a continual basis.

5. Avoid buying plants that are infested with snails.

Proper Lighting

Adequate lighting is undoubtedly the most important aspect of maintaining live plants in an aquarium system. As a general rule, dark green plants will survive at lower light levels than pale green or reddish colored species, which will need more light to achieve proper growth. The lighting system that you choose will play an important role as to which plants you will be able to keep successfully.

How Plants Use Light to Make Food

Good lighting is required for the process of photosynthesis. During photosynthesis, plants synthesize carbohydrates and carbon dioxide from the water through chlorophyll pigment cells to produce food. Plants acquire a majority of their food in this manner.

THE RIGHT AMOUNT OF LIGHT

If you want your plants to achieve maximum growth and health, you will need to provide at least 1.5 watts of fluorescent light per gallon of water for eight to twelve hours per day. In most cases, two fluorescent strip lights will completely illuminate your tank. Metal halide bulbs, which supply very intense wavelengths, are an alternative. The disadvantages to metal halide lighting are that it can be very expensive and may provide too much light if the tank is not heavily planted. No matter which lighting you choose, it's always wise to use a timing device to supply your tank with a consistent level of light each day.

BULBS

When selecting lighting tubes, make sure they are full spectrum or "grow lights." This will ensure that your plants are supplied with the red, blue and yellow spectrums that aren't available in adequate

amounts on standard cool white florescent or incandescent fixtures. Standard house lights should never be used on an aquarium because they won't provide the correct spectrums that are needed for plant growth.

To keep plants well-anchored, you will want to lay a substrate about two inches in depth.

Plants in the Aquarium

Plants do not usually live in complete isolation. Like any other living creature, they must be able to interact correctly with their environment.

THE RIGHT SUBSTRATE

An aquarium's substrate has a strong effect on plant growth. Gravel that is 1½ to 2 inches deep will successfully hold down your plant's roots. If not enough substrate is present, your plants will have a difficult time anchoring themselves. Plants absorb most of their nutrients through their roots, so the correct depth of substrate is essential to their survival.

Remember that undergravel filters can rob plants of needed nutrients. If your system is set up with an undergravel filter, you can use clay flowerpots to house your plants. Periodic pruning will also allow healthy leaves to absorb more nutrients.

COMBINING FISH AND LIVE PLANTS

Not all fish are suitable for heavily planted aquariums. Some species of fish will eat your plants or uproot them while digging around in the substrate. Luckily, discus do not munch on leaves or dig very often. The fish population in your aquarium should also be kept at a minimum so that you do not overload the tank's holding capacity or distract from the natural beauty of a planted tank. Also, large, densely planted tanks will leave less free-swimming areas for your fish.

> ### AN ALTERNATIVE DESIGN
>
> A bare bottom tank without live plants, gravel or any type of decorations is an alternative setup for your discus. This method helps to provide an immaculate water environment because it is easier to clean a tank without any obstructions. Bare tanks are often used for breeding. However, the appearance of a bare tank is usually less pleasing to the eye and is less cozy for your fish than an aquarium that is set up with live plants and substrate.

The water parameters of your live plants and fish must match in order for both to remain healthy and happy. A discus aquarium usually has a water temperature between 80° and 85°F, and a pH level of 6.5. An acidic environment and warm water conditions will limit your choices in live plants because many tropical species will turn brown and die in this type of system. However, there are a few plants that will survive well in a discus aquarium.

POPULAR PLANTS FOR THE DISCUS AQUARIUM

The following list will give you a few good ideas as to which types of plants can live safely in your discus aquarium. Tall plants should be placed along the rear of the glass, and shorter ones up front. Make sure to leave enough space between each plant so that they can grow properly, and do not push any species into the substrate deeper than the crown (the area right above the roots).

Amazon Sword (Echinodorus bleheri)

Amazon swords are tall and have large, thick leaves that are ideal for placement along the back of the aquarium. The Amazon sword is without a doubt the most popular aquarium flora. The Amazon sword is a fast-growing plant that prefers high light intensities. A single plant can grow more than fifty leaves. After flowering, new small plants will develop on the peduncle, which can be cut off and replanted in the substrate.

Banana Plants (Nymphoides aquatica)

Banana plants are native to Florida and have heart-shaped leaves that are attached to long,

By placing tall plants in the rear of the tank, you won't obscure the view of your fish.

slender stems. Small green bananas often appear on the bottom of this plant and may grow up to two inches in length. These tiny bananas can either be placed under the substrate or left partially exposed. Leaves may be trimmed and allowed to grow until they bloom into another plant. The bananas store nutrients, and are actually a part of the root system.

Cabomba (Cabomba furcata)

Hobbyists are often fascinated by the red-brown appearance of the cabomba plant and its finely dis-sected leaves. The red (sometimes purple) flower is carried on a floating leaf. The cabomba requires very soft and slightly acidic water, intense lighting and prefers a nutrient-rich substrate. If aquarium condi-tions are poor, the plant will decay. If provided with a suitable environment, cabomba will grow very quickly.

Hornwort (Ceratophylum demersum)

Hornwort is probably the most hardy of all the bunched plant species, and can easily adapt to different water parameters. This species is great for providing shelter for females and young fry. Hornwort can be planted or free-floating.

Java Fern (Microsorium pteropus)

The java fern is native to Africa, and can be found on land as well as in water. This is a beautiful tropical plant that has broad green leaves. This species is very tough and hardy, and is perfect for beginning aquarists. Java fern leaves have an unpleasant taste and are rarely eaten by aquarium fish. This species will tolerate a wide range of water conditions, and can be attached to a piece of driftwood or rock with a rubber band. When the band eventually deteriorates in the water, the plant will have already developed a root system to anchor itself.

Plants with long, tall leaves are ideal for placement at the back of your aquarium.

Red Ludwigia (Ludwigia glandulosa)

Ludwigia is a very attractive bunch plant. This species has bright red color patterns on the underside of its green leaves. Popular and hardy, the ludwigia plant requires bright lighting to maintain its intense color, and will add beauty to your discus aquarium when placed in the foreground areas of the tank.

Water Sprite (Ceratopteris thalicroides)

Water sprite is a rooted plant that can grow very tall, and has brilliant emerald green foliage. This species can be either floating or rooted in form, and will reproduce by producing buds or spores. The water sprite is found throughout the tropics, and requires bright light and moderately warmer temperatures.

Other Good Plants

In nature, there are several plants that will grow naturally on tree roots or small stones. The *Anubias*, *Microsorum pteropus*, *Bolibitis* and the *Vesicularia dubyana* have a special root system known as "crampons," which they use to anchor themselves to small rocks or pieces of wood. These plants tolerate a wide range of light and do well in most water conditions.

Purchasing Live Plants

A few aquarium supply shops sell live plants, and many chain-based pet stores carry a wide variety of assorted tropical plants at a very reasonable price. If there's no store in your area, you can always purchase plants through Internet-based Web sites and mail-order advertisements found in fish-keeping magazines.

TRANSPORTING PLANTS

Make sure that your plants don't dry out on the way home from the pet shop. You can keep them moist by asking your dealer to bag them in water or carefully wrap each one in wet newspaper. While in the car, carry your new plants in a Styrofoam cooler so that the water will remain warm. On arrival, place your new plants in a shallow pan of water that contains a 10 percent solution of potassium permanganate for disinfecting. Trim cuttings to the correct length for you tank, and remove any dead or wilted leaves using a sharp pair of scissors.

Feeding Your Plants

Tablets and liquid feeders can be placed in the gravel near the plant's roots for fertilization. "Plant plugs" can provide nutrition for your plants on a continual basis. Single cuttings can be placed in the center of each plug, and then buried in the substrate.

Keeping Plants Healthy

Should your plants fail, you need to evaluate the cause. If your plant leaves turn yellow, they are probably suf-

fering from iron deficiency. You can add some fertilizer to correct this problem. If the leaves are yellow with green veins, they will need trace elements as well. Black or brown leaves indicate that the plant has been overfed with iron. To keep your plants healthy, perform regular water changes to keep nitrates low, add a well-balanced fertilizer periodically and make sure that your lighting remains constant.

Aquarium plants, like your fish, will do best if frequent water changes are performed.

Aquascaping Your Aquarium

To keep your discus healthy and happy, you can re-create scenes from their natural environment in your aquarium. In fact, studying the natural environment of any species will help you to plan the aquascaping that you'll want to use in their tank. This is known as setting up a biotope tank or natural environment aquarium.

DRIFTWOOD

For natural beauty and color, you can purchase driftwood or bog wood to create a biotope tank. Discus are usually found in the wild regions of the Amazon where they use tree trunks, roots and piles of driftwood for refuge. Driftwood can be arranged to form caves and resting places, and requires little maintenance.

Natural driftwood can cause the aquarium water to turn a yellowish brown or tea color, and may drop the pH into a slightly acidic range. This is a safe and natural softening process that will release natural tannins into the water. Small pieces of driftwood can be piled up in the foreground of the tank, and larger pieces can be attached to the back wall of the aquarium with suction cups. Some pieces of driftwood available in pet supply shops will already have the suction cups installed, or will be mounted to a base plate.

Driftwood will also provide a safe refuge for your discus. Large pieces of this material can be costly, but are well worth the investment because they are very durable and will last a long time.

ROCK AND STONE FORMATIONS

All rocks and stones should be cleansed and disinfected before introducing them into the tank in order to kill any parasites or other unwelcome inhabitants. One good way to disinfect rocks is by boiling or by soaking them in a mild bleach solution. After bleaching, rinse the rocks in clear water and allow them to air dry for at least twenty-four hours prior to placing them into the tank. If you don't want to collect your own, many pet shops stock various assortments of precleaned rocks.

Most rocks have no direct affect on the pH balance of aquarium water. If you do suspect problems with a particular rock and its effect on water chemistry, you can place it in a holding tank and then test the water after a few days to check fluctuations in the pH level before adding it to your aquarium.

Driftwood and rocks make attractive accents to the aquarium, and provide your fish with a place to hide.

PLASTIC PLANTS

There are a number of top quality plastic plants that look real and will add a nice splash of color to your discus tank. Most artificial plants are reasonably priced, and the selection is quite varied. When adding artificial plants (just like live ones) be sure to thoroughly wash them before you put them into your aquarium system.

DON'T GET CARRIED AWAY

No matter which setup you choose, be careful not to overload the tank with a lot of decorations. Discus are carnivorous by nature, and will make a real mess at dinnertime. Uneaten food can easily go unnoticed in a heavily decorated tank, and will begin to decay when it is allowed to remain in the water for any length of time. Excessive tank decorations can make cleanup and regular water changes difficult.

Substrate

Substrates are used to create a natural-looking environment. The natural substrate for discus in the Amazon

consists of fine gravel and mud. Mud is not recommended for use in the home aquarium because it would ruin even the finest filtration system. It's important to remember that the color and choice of substrate should complement the beautiful colors of your discus. Brightly colored substrates will over-

Substrates that are neutral in color with smooth edges are best for the discus tank.

power and take away from the natural setting that you are trying to re-create. It's better to stick with natural-colored (earth-based) tones. Some discus can be shy by nature, and bright gravel will keep them in a constant nervous state.

SUBSTRATE SIZE

It's important to choose gravel that cannot easily fit into the small mouth of your discus. Although discus aren't generally known to be avid diggers, they often rummage through the gravel in search of an extra meal. Small stones can be swallowed and cause injury. Any substrate that you purchase should have smooth edges to prevent damage to their delicate mouth region.

Backgrounds

The back wall of the discus aquarium should be covered with some type of scenery, which you can find at most pet supply shops. Backgrounds are manufactured to fit any size tank and offer a wide variety of color schemes and pictures to choose from. By covering the back glass, you can create a cave-like environment that's pleasing to you, and will allow your discus to feel more secure. After adding a background, you'll notice a higher concentration of light within the tank, and extra light will benefit any live plants that you have.

Another option is to paint the back wall on the outside of the tank before you set it up. Avoid painting the glass with darker colors such as black and brown, which will make your fish difficult to see. Green, turquoise and light blue colors offer a peaceful and pleasant appearance. A painted background will also cut down on glare and add to the beauty of fish photos. The paint can be easily removed with a razor blade if you decide to return the tank to its original clear condition.

Maintenance Equipment

There are several other items that you'll need on hand for daily, weekly and monthly maintenance procedures.

BUCKETS

A plastic container, such as a bucket or water pail, will help with water changes. A bucket can be used for holding water as you clean the tank with a gravel cleaner and siphon hose. Make sure that you rinse the pail after each trip so that clean water will be placed back into the tank.

GRAVEL VACUUM

Gravel vacuums are manufactured in a wide variety of different sizes and can be manually operated, electrically driven or battery-powered. A gravel vacuum is a great tool for cleaning loose particles of uneaten food and fish waste that have become buried along the top of the gravel bed. Periodically vacuuming your aquarium will clean out a lot of fine debris that cannot be removed from the tank by the filtration equipment.

NETS

It's wise to have a separate net for each aquarium that you have in operation, in order to prevent cross-contamination of germs between your tanks. Periodically, you'll need to cleanse your nets in a dip solution (which you can purchase at the pet store) and then rinse them in clear water before using them again. Make sure to use the proper size net for each individual species to avoid damaging the fish's fins, scales or slime coat.

WHY SOME PLANTS CAN'T LIVE IN A DISCUS SYSTEM

Chlorophyll is a complex liquid that enables a plant to possess green coloration and make its own food through photosynthesis. Pyrrole is a related plant liquid that is soluble in a weak solution of acid-based water. When the acidic condition of an aquarium exceeds the required minimum strength of a particular species of plant, it removes pyrrole from the leaves of the plant and releases it into the water. If the pyrrole is removed at a rate that is faster than the plant can produce it, the chlorophyll will fade and turn brown from lack of nutrients. The plant will then die from starvation.

pH LEVEL TEST KITS

Low level test kits are used for monitoring the lower acidic levels of water that are usually present in a discus tank environment. Low level kits are designed to test and monitor the acidic to slight alkaline levels between 6.0 to 6.9 on the pH scale. A standard pH test kit often contains a plastic tube that is filled with aquarium water and a reagent solution, and is then matched against a color card.

To be on the safe side, have a high level test kit as well. This kit is effective in testing pH levels between the range of 7.2 to 8.8. If your pH jumps into the high range, you'll need this kit to monitor water conditions until you can bring it back down to a proper acidic level.

Electronic pH Meter

If you want the ultimate tool for checking your pH levels without the hassle of a test tube or strip paper, you might consider purchasing an electronic pH meter. Electronic meters are very easy to use and can cover the entire pH range, without having to purchase separate kits. An electronic meter's probe, which produces a digital reading of the current pH, is inserted into the aquarium water.

Ammonia Test Kit

You'll want to monitor the ammonia levels in a new tank setup during the cycling period. You can also use this kit to monitor ammonia levels that may rise periodically from fouling by excess food particles that have not been removed from the system, overfeeding or allowing a dead fish to remain in the tank for any period of time. Ammonia is one of the deadliest toxins found in aquarium water, and your tank should be monitored regularly for any high concentrations that can lead to disease and death.

Nitrite and Nitrate Test Kits

Nitrites and nitrates are toxins that are produced from a chemical breakdown of ammonia. A nitrite and nitrate test kit will help to monitor water conditions during and after the cycling period. If testing reveals a high level of nitrites or nitrates, a water change will quickly lower them to a safer level.

Chlorine and Chloramine Test Kit

This kit can be used each time you perform a water change to test the concentrations of chlorine or chloramines, which are ammonia-based products. If chloramines are present, be sure to check and make sure that your dechlorinator is capable of removing or neutralizing them.

Caring
for

part three

Discus

chapter 7

Bringing
Your Discus
Home

Until recently, discus were very limited in availability and were difficult to find at local fish shops. When the discus was first introduced into the hobby, it was captured from the wild in the Amazon territory and then imported to retail markets around the world. During that particular time, there were only five species available, which were commonly known as the Wild Heckle discus, Pineapple discus, green discus, brown discus and the blue discus.

Today, there are hundreds of discus varieties to choose from due to the captive- and hybrid-bred strains that have been produced by thousands of breeders around the world. Discus are commonly chosen by color or fin type.

Finding Discus

SPECIALTY SHOPS

Discus can usually be found in some of the more reputable pet stores that have dedicated a majority of their livestock to species aquariums. Shops that focus on maintaining different species of tropical fish will generally have tanks set up that supply the proper water parameters for each species. It is in this type of specialty shop that you will usually find a good selection of healthy discus.

MAIL-ORDER SERVICES AND HATCHERIES

You may also use a mail-order service to purchase your fish directly from a hatchery. Hatcheries are located throughout the world, and are enjoying an increasing popularity among hobbyists and breeders. Most reputable hatcheries can be easily located on the World Wide Web.

Some hatcheries will deliver to your nearest airport, while others will deliver to your door. Mail-order service is very reliable, and most of these hatcheries will include a live fish guarantee to protect you financially if the fish are lost during the shipping process. The only drawback to ordering discus through a mail-order service is that you can't handpick the fish of your choice like you could if you bought them in your local area. However, Internet Web sites usually provide photos of the discus for sale.

FIVE GREAT REASONS TO KEEP DISCUS

1. Discus are one of the most desired and sought after fish within the hobby.

2. Discus have unique natural beauty and grace not found in other fish.

3. Discus have many colors and fin styles to choose from.

4. Discus are calm, soothing, sensitive and interesting to watch.

5. Demand is high for quality home-bred discus.

Purchasing Discus

If you're new to keeping discus, you may want to start with a more hardy species, such as the Pigeon Blood or Red Turquoise varieties, that are easy for beginning hobbyists to work with. Hybrid strains of discus have been developed within the confines of the aquarium breeder's realm and have become accustomed to various types of water conditions in comparison to fish found in their natural habitat. Hybrids can be kept by beginning aquarium hobbyists without previous discus experience. The

hybrid species have adapted to many different ranges of domesticated water supplies and are not quite as demanding as wild strains.

WILD STRAINS

You may want to eventually work with a more temperamental species of discus after you've gained a little insight, hands-on experience and knowledge on how to properly take care of them. These wild strains are really not delicate or fragile, they just require more exacting water conditions in order to keep them in an environment that is similar to the natural habitat from which they were taken.

YOUNGER DISCUS

If possible, you should purchase younger discus (2 to 3 inches) because they are not as prone to stress as full-grown adults and tend to be more economical in price.

Putting It All Together

Remember, the main key to being successful in keeping discus is to first start by purchasing healthy specimens (see Chapter 3), and then provide them with proper nutrition and a natural environment in which to live. If you follow these three simple guidelines, you won't have problems keeping and maintaining a beautiful and healthy colony of discus.

Transporting Your Discus

One of the most common mistakes that new hobbyists make is to overlook proper transportation procedures when they are moving their new discus from one location to another. The transportation period can be one of the most stressful events that your new aquatic pets will encounter. If there is not a lot of travel time involved between the dealer and your home, few problems occur. But if a long period of travel is involved, there are a few things that you can do to help prepare them for their journey home.

BEFORE YOU LEAVE THE STORE

The first thing that you want to do before you leave the store is to request that the clerk double-bag your fish for safety. If the first bag happened to get punctured at the store and went unnoticed, the second bag would prevent water loss on the way home. A fish's fins also frequently puncture bags if it becomes startled during transportation and starts darting around in its container.

It's also a good idea to request that no more than two fish be placed in each bag. Overcrowding discus in small amounts of water can become dangerous on long trips because ammonia release can build up to toxic proportions in a relatively short period of time.

> ### DON'T FREAK OUT
>
> Discus will often lie on their side just moments after being placed inside of a plastic holding bag. The first time that you personally experience this strange phenomenon, you may be startled into believing that your new fish has died. Don't be alarmed, as this is a common resting position for transported discus.

STRESS RELIEF PRODUCTS

Stress Coat can be placed in a transportation bag to help relieve stress from quickly deteriorating water conditions that often arise during a long transition period from the dealer to your home aquarium.

USING A STYROFOAM COOLER AND HEAT PACKS

There is another simple tool that you can use to help comfort your fish while they are being transported. A small Styrofoam cooler placed on the back seat can conveniently carry fish bags and prevent them from rolling around inside of the vehicle or falling onto the floorboard.

HEAT PACKS

Heat packs can be put inside of the Styrofoam cooler if you are anticipating a long drive. The heat packs will keep the water warm and prevent the fish from becoming sick from chilling. Heat packs are often used during cooler weather, and can be purchased at most sporting goods stores that carry hunting equipment. Many hatcheries won't ship their discus during cooler seasons because the heat packs may fail on extremely long journeys and result in needless fish losses.

Your discus will be happiest in a comfortable tank— not a plastic bag! So get your fish home as quickly as possible.

PORTABLE OXYGEN

A bottle of portable oxygen can come in handy if you have a long road to travel. You can periodically add a shot of oxygen to the bags in order to replenish that which has been lost. Of course, a one-hour ride certainly would not require you to use this element. A much simpler option is to purchase a battery-operated air pump. A small airstone can be carefully inserted into a plastic jug with your discus. This pump will allow for better gas exchange during the trip.

TRANSPORTATION TIME FRAMES

Most discus can survive in an enclosed plastic bag (which contains oxygen) from twenty-four to twenty-eight hours without developing problems. If you go to your local pet shop to buy fish, the oxygen in the bag would provide you with more than enough time to safely transport your new aquatic pets home. If your pet shop does not fill the bag with oxygen, you'll have a few hours before you really start pushing it to the limit. Higher temperatures will also shorten this safety time frame. Always purchase your fish right before you're ready to go home. If you have other shopping planned, do that first.

The Acclimation Period

The acclimation process is the period of time that it takes for your new fish to adjust or acclimate themselves to your aquarium. The acclimation process will allow your new discus to get used to the temperature, pH level and hardness of the water. Proper acclimation procedures will help them to blend into their new environment without being shocked or stressed, and will provide a safer transition from the plastic bags to their new aquarium.

Know Your pH Levels

The first step in acclimating your fish is to make sure that the pH levels of the water in the bag and the tank match each other. If there is a big difference between the two pH values, you'll need to make some adjustments in your water chemistry to bring both levels within two-tenths (.2) of each other before your fish can actually be placed in the tank. This process can easily be performed days or even weeks before purchase if you have already decided on which supplier

> **TEMPERATURE TIP**
>
> A thermometer placed in the dealer's plastic bag will keep you posted on the internal temperature so that you can prevent shock and know when the two water sources are equalized.

you will be using. You can ask your dealer about the pH levels in his holding tanks, and then adjust your aquarium water to the same level before you bring the fish home.

Lights Out

While acclimating new arrivals, turn all of the aquarium lights off before you float the bags in the water.

This will reduce stress and keep your new discus from being picked on by any other inhabitants.

FLOATING THE BAGS

The third step involved in acclimation is to let the newly acquired fish float inside the tank, which will

bring the temperature in the bag to the same level as the aquarium water. If you float the bag with its top open, you can slowly add the tank water to it. In most cases, the bag temperature will be several degrees lower than the main tank.

Place the discus bags into the tank and let them float for thirty minutes. This will allow the temperature inside the bag to gradually become warmer. After thirty minutes have passed, add one cup of water from the tank into each bag. This will begin to adjust both pH and temperatures levels. You can use a clothespin or a bag clip to reseal the bag instead of the rubber bands commonly used by most pet stores. This will allow you to open and close the bags with ease. Continue this cycle until the conditions in the bag match those in the main tank.

Minimize the trauma of entering the tank by turning off the lights as you introduce your new arrival.

DRIP METHODS

A more technical way of acclimating discus or any other type of tropical fish to its new aquarium is by using a drip method. If you can gain access to an IV pole and IV bag (the type that are used in medical facilities) you can place the tank water into the IV bag and allow it to drip directly into the fish bags while they float in the aquarium. This method will allow the new discus to acclimate at a much slower rate without being stressed from quick fluctuations in water parameters.

OBSERVE YOUR FISH

Watch your fish through the acclimation process. Look for any changes in behavior such as rapid breathing, odd positioning and other signs of distress. If the new fish seem uncomfortable or disturbed, allow the bag to float for another thirty minutes and add a stress relief product. After signs of improvement have been noted, you may release the fish into its new environment.

RELEASE METHODS

There are several ways to release fish into the tank. Some hobbyists prefer to net their fish and place them into the tank so that none of the water from the pet shop enters the new aquarium (to protect against disease). This procedure is pretty common but can cause fin damage to the fish. Other hobbyists prefer not to risk stressing their fish with a net, and will open the bag to allow the discus to swim out on its own. An alternative method is to fill a large plastic glass with water from the tank and set it by a sink in your home. Take the discus bag to the sink and drain almost all of the water out of it and then slide the fish into the plastic container. Next, take the container to the main tank and slowly lower it into the water so that the discus can freely swim out of the container.

If you take care in transporting and acclimating your discus, your fish will be relaxed in its new home.

THE FIRST TWENTY-FOUR HOURS

After you've added the discus to the tank, you may want to observe them for a while to monitor their behavior in their new environment. You can expect them to be very shy at first, and they may hide for the first few days. Keep the lights in the tank off for at least twenty-four hours to provide security and a less startling environment for them until they fully adjust to their new surroundings.

Feeding should not be attempted on the first day because they will probably not want to eat until they feel comfortable. If you insist on feeding, try a small pinch of flake food, and refrain from offering live or frozen foods until they have become fully adjusted to the new tank.

GETTING USED TO PEOPLE

Your fish will have to make adjustments to their new environment when placed into your home aquarium. The first adjustment is to the aquarium itself and their new tankmates. If any other fish become aggressive toward the new arrivals, you can change the decorations around to break up previously defined territories. In addition, your discus needs to become familiar with you and any other people that are living in your home. Approach the tank slowly for the first few days so that you don't startle them.

Sit Back and Enjoy

If you take the time to purchase healthy fish, transport them safely and acclimate them properly, you'll quickly be able to sit back and enjoy your new happy and healthy aquatic friends.

chapter 8

Feeding
Your
Discus

A recommended diet for your discus would consist of brine shrimp, daphnia, flake foods, spirulina, plankton, worms and insects. All foods should be continually rotated so that a good variety is achieved. Feedings should also be alternated on a daily basis in order to provide a balanced source of proteins, vitamins, carbohydrates and other natural substances. Your discus will

quickly become bored if it's forced to eat the same foods every day. In fact, some fish have been known to completely stop eating when offered the same meals day after day.

Types of Foods for Your Discus

LIVE FOOD

The best way to locate live food is through the Internet because many aquarium shops do not carry it. Four premium live foods that can be found on the World Wide Web include brine shrimp, water fleas, white worms and very small silversides. Some hobbyists tend to shy away from feeding their discus live food. But the

fact remains, in the wild, fish eat insects, worms and other fish. Live food is an important part of the natural food chain.

Live foods such as tubifex or bloodworms should be avoided, as they may carry parasites. Earthworms are a very good source of food that you can probably find in your neighborhood.

Rinse off earth-worms well before offering them to your discus.

Rinse all worms with clear water before feeding to eliminate any fertilizers or insecticides. When feeding this type of worm, you will need to cut or chop them up into small pieces before offering them to your discus.

FROZEN FOODS

Frozen foods such as brine shrimp, krill, plankton, daphnia, and white mosquito larvae are considered acceptable fare, and are usually processed in a sanitary environment. There are also mixtures of frozen diets on the market that are packaged especially for discus and are high in protein and enriched with vitamins. Make sure that you rinse all frozen foods well before feeding them to your fish.

When using frozen or live foods, there will always be some portions of the food that won't be eaten. That's why it's so important to feed live foods sparingly. Uneaten live foods can create foul water conditions, and they should be removed in a timely manner so that they are not left to decay within the tank. As with most

82

cichlids, discus are messy eaters and will not clean everything off of their aquatic plate.

COMMERCIAL FLAKES AND PELLETS

Flake foods are an exceptional staple food and are readily accepted by most discus. Larger flakes are recommended for adults, and smaller flakes (which become saturated at a faster rate) can be used if you're feeding juveniles. Some pellet foods have become very popular among hobbyists and have been formulated especially for discus.

Some commercial fish food is formulated just for discus. Make sure that the food you choose is appropriate for the size of your fish.

Beware of inexpensive fish food that is sold in bulk. Bulk food found in pet supply stores may be aged to the point where it has lost much of its nutritional value. As with any other endeavor, you get what you pay for. Stick with dry food that's sealed in small containers so that you know you are purchasing a fresh product.

FREEZE-DRIED FOODS

Freeze-dried foods usually contain a mixture of small crustaceans, shrimp and worms that are well preserved and vacuum packed. Freeze-dried foods are great for a periodic treat or change of pace.

MAIL-ORDER FISH FOOD

There are many discus hatcheries that also sell mail-order food, which is usually prepared and manufactured within their facilities. Many hatcheries will also offer a speedy mail-order service when you purchase their product.

Making Your Own Discus Food

Mixing up homemade discus food has become a popular activity among hobbyists. Making your own discus food will allow you to prepare aquatic meals in large amounts for a very economical price. These meals can be conveniently frozen for later use.

83

Another advantage of making your own recipes is that you can add vitamins, extra protein, vegetables and even medications if they are needed. There are many different ways to create discus food, and recipes are only limited by the imagination. The following recipe will give you one good mixture of ingredients that will provide your discus with a well-balanced treat. This recipe is not intended to be used as a staple, but can be implemented into your feeding schedule as an alternative to the wide variety of dry and live foods that you usually offer.

Discus Delight

A wonderful treat for your discus.

Ingredients:

3 fresh eggs
5 oz. frozen green peas
1 lb. frozen shrimp
1 lb. fish fillets (skinless/boneless and
  avoid fatty fish meats)
5 oz. frozen carrots
1 fresh banana
5 oz. frozen chopped spinach
½ lb. frozen crabmeat
10 aquatic multivitamins
10 oz. aquarium flake food

Preparation:

Place the eggs, spinach, peas and carrots in a bowl and microwave them for three minutes. (Make sure that you use a microwave-safe bowl!) Next, place the finely chopped shrimp, fish fillets and crabmeat in a pot of boiling water and let it cook for two minutes.

Place all of the previously cooked ingredients into a blender and add the vitamin tablets, flake food and a peeled banana.

Blend all ingredients until the mixture is of even consistency. If the contents become too pasty, add a small amount of water to thin it out. If the mixture is too watery, add a little more flake food until the desired consistency is reached.

Place the blended food into food storage bags and lay them on a cutting board. Carefully press down on the sides of each bag until the mixture inside is flat. Put each bag in the freezer. Never refreeze any food after it has been thawed. Food will lose its nutritional value, and may spoil if refrozen. If you need just a small piece for a treat, simply break off a chunk from the main sheet and place it in the aquarium. As it floats on the top of the water, your discus will really enjoy nibbling on it.

PROPER FOOD STORAGE

Storing aquatic foods properly will help to keep them fresh and full of nutrients for a long period of time. Improper storage can result in spoilage and lost nutrients. Dry foods such as flakes and pellets can be kept in the refrigerator to help keep them fresh. Frozen foods should be kept in the freezer and carefully wrapped to prevent freezer burn.

You can separate foods into small bags so that the entire contents can be used during a day's feeding to prevent thawing and refreezing of unused food portions. Live worms that will be used to feed your discus can be kept in a container in your refrigerator for freshness.

> **FIVE WAYS TO PROVIDE A NUTRITIOUS DIET**
>
> 1. Offer foods that are high in protein.
> 2. Avoid live foods that are often infested with parasites.
> 3. Feed a variety of different foods at interval feedings.
> 4. Offer vitamin-fortified foods to prevent vitamin deficiencies.
> 5. Do not overfeed.

Components of a Healthy Diet

PROTEINS

Proteins help your fish build strong tissue and muscles. Proteins are found in a diet that includes insects, fish and other live animal foods. Proteins play a very important role in promoting proper physical growth. Younger fish will need a little more protein in their diet than full-grown adults.

VITAMINS

Vitamins can be supplied by providing a diet that combines a good balance of preprocessed and live foods. A balanced diet will include vitamin A (found in eggs, greens and crustaceans), vitamin B (found in algae, fish and greens), vitamin C (found in algae), vitamin D (found in algae, shrimp and worms), vitamin E (found in algae and eggs), vitamin H (found in liver and eggs) and vitamin K (found in greens and liver).

Animal foods contain protein, which is critical to building your discus' muscles.

MINERALS AND CARBOHYDRATES

Minerals are important for proper growth, and can be provided in liquid form. Another way to administer minerals is through frequent water changes. Carbohydrates will provide energy and help your discus resist disease, but may be harmful if fed to excess levels.

FOODS THAT CONTAIN ANIMAL FAT

It's not a good idea to feed your discus foods that contain large amounts of animal fat because it's not easily digested. These types of foods often result in gastric disorders, which can have adverse effects and cause death in some species. Animal fat (which is not found in abundance in discus' natural diet) remains unabsorbed in the digestive track and eventually blocks the gastric system. The best type of meat that you can feed your discus is the flesh of other fish. The oils found in fish are different from animal meat and can be easily digested.

How to Feed Your Discus

Before you offer any type of food to your new aquatic pet, make sure to turn the aquarium lights on and allow the fish to wake up or adjust to their environment. Discus are not nocturnal feeders, and should be fed during the daylight hours.

If you are going to offer a late-night feeding or snack, make sure that you allow your discus enough time to complete their natural rummaging and foraging excursions before you give them any more food. Discus will often clean up uneaten particles from a previous meal if given time. A short waiting period will ensure that most of the food has been eaten, and has not been left to decay on the tank floor.

Turn on lights and give your fish a chance to wake up and smell the coffee before you add food to the tank.

HOW MUCH SHOULD YOU FEED?

As a general rule in feeding tropical fish, you should never feed them more than they can consume within a five-minute period. If your discus are still roaming the tank in search of food after the five minutes have expired, they're probably still hungry. You should offer enough food to satisfy their increased appetite, but only a little at a time so that you can keep track of what's been left untouched. A discus has a stomach that is smaller than its eye, so you might want to keep that in mind when it's constantly begging for extra food.

HOW OFTEN SHOULD YOU FEED?

Adult discus should be fed two or three times a day. Small juvenile discus can be fed up to five times a day to promote proper growth patterns. It's much better to feed several small meals periodically throughout the day than to dump a whole bunch of food in at one time. Small meals will allow your discus to digest its

meal before the next feeding. One large meal will only
fill it up once a day. The remainder of the time, it will
be very hungry.

OVERFEEDING

Overfeeding is caused by not properly measuring the
food that is offered at each individual feeding. You
often hear hobbyists say that you should give your fish
just a small "pinch" of food. But exactly how much is a
single pinch? Depending on your hand and finger size,
a pinch can turn out to be a little bit of food or a lot of
grub. Beginning hobbyists may not be able to automatically determine how much is considered the correct amount to feed.

Sometimes fish keepers think that if a little bit of nour-
ishment is good, maybe a lot will be even better.

Overfeeding can cause ammonia
to build up quickly and cause toxic
situations within the tank's water.
One classic sign of overfeeding is
cloudy, fouled water, which can
turn deadly if uneaten food is
allowed to remain on the tank
floor to decay. Overfeeding should
always be avoided at all costs.

PREMEASURE

The safest way to feed is by pre-
measuring each serving. Feed your
discus for a few days to see how
much it can eat in a five-minute period of time. Place
individual servings in plastic bags, and feed directly from
them. Using this method, you will be able to avoid the
temptation of putting extra food into the aquarium.

*The little mouth
of the discus can
only manage
finely chopped
foods.*

FOOD PREPARATIONS

A discus is incapable of eating large pieces of food
because of its small mouth structure. Chopping or
crushing larger foods will be required when preparing
certain meals. A small blender or food processor can

also be used to make the food more acceptable in size, and will come in handy if you ever want to make your own blends of fish food at home.

Feeding and Observation

Feeding your discus always provides a great opportunity for you to sit back and carefully monitor their physical health and social activity. If your discus are colorful, vigorous and have a good appetite, they are probably in excellent condition. If all members of the tank feed together in relative harmony, there are probably not any social problems to concern yourself with.

Because fish often defecate after feeding, close observation can reveal any signs of intestinal troubles such as loose, whitish feces. Close observation will also allow you to carefully monitor any overfeeding problems, so that you can make adjustments at the next scheduled feeding.

> **ASH ALERT**
>
> Ash is an ingredient that is often found in premanufactured fish food. Ash is inorganic and contains pulverized pieces of fish bone and scales. Manufacturers are beginning to reduce the total amount of ash in their products because it may foul water and be harmful to aquarium fish. Check the can's label for ash levels in food products, or call the manufacturer if the content is not listed on the container.

Variety Is the Spice of Life

Discus are omnivores, eating both animal and vegetable substances. In their native habitat, they feed on insects and vegetables. They're also known to eat fish fry if they're small enough to fit into their mouth.

A Picky Eater

Some discus can be picky eaters at meal times unless they are being offered familiar food. Foods that can be found in their native habitat will usually become their favorite meal. If you're going to introduce a new type of food, you may want to slowly accustom your fish to it by mixing it in with standard fare until the discus develop a taste for the new food.

Overeaters

A fish can become obese if it consistently eats more than it needs. Fish that have become disfigured in size due to overfeeding are not in good health. Obese fish tend to suffer physically due to the overexertion caused by excessive weight.

Feeding Newborn Fry

Discus fry will feed off of a special coating on their parent's skin during their first week of life. Both parents secrete a product called discus milk, which forms a coat on their skin. If the parents neglect their fry (this happens once in a blue moon), they will have to be fed on a substitute formula, which consists of making a paste from dried eggs. Using this method, the young fry are placed in a shallow pan, and the paste is smeared on the walls along the water's edge. Because the small pan has to be cleaned between each feeding, it is better to leave the young fry with their parents.

Newborn discus will consume discus milk secreted by the parents. After that time, you need to take over as the food provider.

Feeding Young Discus

After the first week has passed, small frozen baby brine or live baby brine should be introduced into the youngster's diet. As they grow larger, other small types of foods, such as flakes and finely chopped foods, should be introduced.

MICROWORMS

Microworms can be cultured at home to feed young fry. To start a culture, mix oatmeal, water and microworms from an existing culture (which you can purchase from dealers found on the Internet or borrow from another hobbyist), and then let it stand in a bowl at room temperature for forty-eight hours. After two days have passed, small worms will appear on the sides of the bowl and can be transferred to the fry tank.

Home Alone!

If you're going away on vacation, you'll need to make arrangements to have someone feed your pets while you are away. Perhaps a trusted family member, a neighbor or local hobbyist is willing to learn how to feed your fish and will take over while you're away. If you don't know anyone who can help out, an alternative method will have to be used.

AUTOMATIC FEEDERS

Automatic feeding stations can be used if you're going to be away from home for a short period of time. A battery-operated or electric feeder will allow you to prepack and automatically distribute a seven-day supply of food. It will also allow you to preset a timed feeding schedule.

Good Nutrition Is Good for Health

With the proper diet and a good environment, your discus will prosper. Nutritional meals will supply your fish with the needed vitamins and minerals to aid in disease prevention and give them an extra boost toward a long and healthy life.

MEDICATED FOODS

Medicated foods have been developed to treat fish that are suffering from internal parasites and other diseases. The internal medication is released as the food is being digested. For this type of medication to be effective, the fish will have to consume the food. Often, sick fish will refuse to eat, and the medicated food will go to waste or be ingested by healthy tankmates.

chapter 9

Keeping
Discus
Healthy

Diseased fish are a problem that all fish keepers will eventually have to face at one time or another. The planet that we live on is saturated with pathogens and parasites. Unfortunately, the underwater world is no exception to this rule. The good news is that most diseases can be cured if they are caught in time.

The best way to take care of your discus' health is by being prepared. Knowing how to properly treat, maintain and prevent disease problems will help you to minimize fish loss and aid in a speedy recovery. The average hobbyist has limited access to scientific instruments such as a microscope, slides and dissecting equipment that could pinpoint and accurately diagnose most diseases. Therefore, fish keepers have to rely on printed material and become familiar with illness by recognizing symptoms and physical ailments that are present during a disease cycle.

Disease Prevention

Prevention is always the best approach in treating any illness. Providing a clean aquatic environment that meets the individual needs of each species is the first step in disease prevention. Aquariums that are kept at less than optimal levels are usually a breeding ground for parasites and pathogens, which unfortunately multiply at a rapid rate.

Discus that are provided with a proper environment will be able to ward off many diseases with a healthy immune system without any intervention on the hobbyist's part. On the other hand, an unhealthy discus can easily become infected

> **BONE UP BEFORE YOU BUY**
>
> The best thing a beginner can do to avoid health problems is to fully study the species of fish he is anticipating on buying long before any purchase is made. Knowing the environment and food that a certain species requires, what diseases are common and how to properly treat them will give you a head start on dealing with health problems if they occur.

with diseases and will not be able to successfully fight off unwanted intruders due to a weakened immune system.

When environmental problems occur, latent disease can manifest quickly and result in a full-blown health problem. A medication called Stress Coat can help with the prevention of certain diseases. A dose of Stress Coat will help to heal tissue that has been damaged by the loss of mucus coating, and will protect against bacteria and fungus attacks. Use Stress Coat when you add new livestock to your tank, or after you have transported them to another aquarium by using a net.

Tank Maintenance Conditions

The majority of diseases are caused by poor water conditions or equipment failure. You should always check the following items before you decide to try any type of medication.

TEMPERATURE

If the temperature in your aquarium is not at the correct level, check to see if your heater is stuck in the on or off position. Adjust the temperature to the correct setting, or replace the heater if you find that it is defective and not working properly.

AERATION

Check your air pump to make sure that there are no obstructions and that it is working correctly. Examine all tubing, airstones and bubble curtains in order to detect any blockages in the airflow.

FILTERS

Filters that have been left unattended for long periods of time may become clogged. If a filter is clogged, it may allow unclean water to be pumped back into the tank. Clean or replace the filter media if it is not functioning properly.

WATER TESTS

Nice clear water is a sign of good water quality in which your discus will thrive.

Evaluate ammonia and nitrate levels periodically. Discus that are exposed to elevated levels of either of these two toxins are weakened and therefore subject to illness. If the tests reveal a high level of ammonia or nitrate, perform an immediate water change to lower the toxins to a safer level.

WATER CLARITY

If your water is consistently cloudy, you should inspect your tank for dead fish. If none are found, check to make sure that the filtration unit is functioning properly. Overfeeding can also cause cloudy water to appear. Cloudy water in an aged aquarium is a sign of fouling, and requires an immediate water change. You can also add an airstone to the aquarium to increase water circulation.

Poor Water Quality

When poor water quality is present, your discus will probably be gasping for air at the surface of the water. If the quality of the water has reached an extremely deteriorated point, your livestock will quickly die if immediate action (water change) is not taken. Tail rot, gill damage and fin rot may be found in a foul water situation. The water can be improved by lowering the pH to the correct level, and performing a large water change of up to 40 percent. Increasing the aeration in the tank with airstones, extra filtration or bubble disks will help to raise the oxygen concentration.

Daily Maintenance for Prevention

There are several things that you can do on a daily basis as part of a preventative maintenance measure to fight against disease. A few minutes a day can save a lot of heartache in the future.

FIVE STEPS TO HEALTHY DISCUS

1. Avoid purchasing any discus that shows signs of sickness or disease.

2. Quarantine a new discus for two weeks before introducing it into the main tank.

3. Maintain top-quality water conditions and a constant temperature.

4. Provide a nutritional diet to boost natural disease defenses.

5. Perform daily maintenance to ensure that all systems are functioning properly.

Maintenance Checklist

1. Monitor the condition of all your equipment, which serves as the life-support system for your aquarium. Check to make sure the filters are functioning properly. If the pads or media are clogged, replace them immediately. Inspect the air pump for optimal output, and make sure that your heater is maintaining the correct temperature.

2. Test water conditions and adjust accordingly. Remove any dead fish, uneaten food or any other foreign substances that could possibly foul the water.

3. Make sure that your aquarium light is putting out maximum illumination. An ample amount of light and an accompanying period of darkness play an important role in your fish's daily health.

Early Detection of Disease

No matter how clean you keep your aquarium, disease will always have a chance to attack your livestock. A clean system reduces the risk but does not eliminate it completely. Many diseases can progress very quickly and should not be allowed to remain untreated. Advanced diseases have the potential to damage the vital organs of your discus to the point where they cannot be healed. Hobbyists should train themselves to make routine aquarium observations so that any drastic changes in physical appearance, social behavior or normal tank activities can be immediately noted and corrected.

By being familiar with your discus' normal appearance and behavior, you're more likely to spot when it's under the weather.

Signs of Illness

The following list will give you a few ideas of what to look for when you are observing your discus and their behavior for signs of illness.

1. Your discus has clamped fins that are kept very close to the body and limit movement.

2. Your discus refuses to eat for more than two days.

3. Your discus is scratching or rubbing against the tank decorations or substrate.

4. Your discus displays bloating or swelling in the abdomen area.

5. Your discus darts around the tank, swims upside down or sideways.

6. Your discus has visible sores, ulcers or physical injuries.

7. Your discus is gasping for air due to gill damage.

8. Your discus develops a continual faded look.

9. Your discus has frayed or ragged fins.

10. Your discus is lying on the bottom of the tank or dangling in corners.

11. Your discus has patchy skin or white spots.

Identifying Diseases

As a beginner, you can gain a lot of valuable information from photographs in books on how to identify disease. You can also consult the dealer at your local pet shop for information and suggestions on how to develop a plan to cure a particular disease.

Specific Treatments

Once you've determined which disease you are dealing with, you can then concentrate on administering precise medical treatments without playing a guessing game. Never dump chemical after chemical into your aquarium in hopes of finding the right cure. Overmedicating can be just as dangerous as not treating the disease at all. Always follow the manufacturer's instructions to the letter, and complete the entire treatment.

Using a Hospital Tank

A hospital tank can be used to treat diseased fish. It is not a good idea to medicate your main display tank because many medication ingredients can damage the biological cycle. The hospital tank should be completely cycled before it is put into use. A seeded sponge filter (preestablished with nitrifying bacteria) from an aged tank can help to speed up the nitrogen cycle.

Setup

A hospital tank should consist of a bare tank (no substrate) with a few plastic plants for comfort. A sponge filter will provide essential biological filtration. Carbon filters can't be used in a hospital tank because they'll destroy the medication or reduce its effectiveness. Lighting in a hospital tank should be kept to a minimum. Raise the temperature of the hospital tank's water by about 5°F (above the setting on the main tank) when treating parasitic infections. Many disease organisms can be eliminated at a quicker rate in warm water.

Water Changes

Regular water changes apply to a hospital tank just as they would to a display tank unless the medication that is being used states otherwise. Medications can be removed from the hospital tank after the treatment process is complete by performing multiple water changes and cleaning the sponge filter.

A water changer can be used to siphon and refill a hospital tank—it works nicely for the main tank, too!

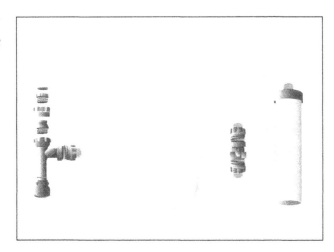

Quarantine Procedures

A quarantine tank will allow you to monitor your newly acquired discus, treat and medicate them if needed and check their overall health before adding them to your established tank. A hospital tank setup can be used for this purpose. Another advantage of quarantining is that you can medicate any illness without having to treat the healthy inhabitants of your main tank. While your new discus is in quarantine, you can evaluate its health and treat diseases that manifest without transmitting the disease to any preexisting tankmates in the main aquarium.

PURCHASING MEDICATIONS

Medications are easily available at any reputable pet supply shop. If the store is closed when you first notice that your livestock is diseased, you can place the afflicted fish in a hospital tank and add a salt treatment of one tablespoon per five gallons of water until you're able to purchase the medication that you need.

Make sure that any medication you use is fresh, and that it is stored in a proper location and at the temperature suggested by the manufacturer. You want to be certain that the product is potent and effective.

Common Fish Medications

Medications commonly used in treating diseased aquarium fish are antibacterial, antifungal or antiparasitic in nature. You should familiarize yourself with each of these products because they are all used to treat different types of diseases.

Noninfectious Diseases

Your discus can show signs of illness that may be caused by noninfectious factors. The following will give you a few ideas about environmentally caused illness.

LACK OF APPETITE

Refusal to eat is usually caused by dominant and aggressive tankmates, introduction to a new tank or poor nutrition.

Treatment—Feed your discus a larger variety of high quality foods and remove dominant tankmates if possible.

POOR WATER QUALITY

Improper water temperatures, inappropriate pH, high levels of ammonia, excessive nitrate and incorrect hardness levels can cause your discus stress.

Treatment—Test all levels and adjust to acceptable readings.

Infectious Diseases and Treatments

Infectious diseases can easily spread to other tankmates if left untreated. If your fish have any of the following illnesses, they should be treated immediately.

POP EYE DISEASE (*EXOPHTHALMIA*)

Protrusion of the eyeball from the eye socket is an obvious symptom of pop eye. The socket is usually inflamed. This disease is often caused by poor water conditions or parasites.

Treatment—An antibiotic such as penicillin capsules should be used as treatment, and the water conditions improved.

TUBERCULOSIS

Tuberculosis (TB) causes your fish to waste away and possess a listless, hollow look. Lesions and ulcers are often present on the body. This is a terminal disease with no known cure, and *this deadly disease can be transmitted to humans.*

Treatment—Euthanize the diseased fish and end its suffering immediately. Wear rubber gloves when removing afflicted fish, and use caution at all times! Never attempt to cure or work with TB-infected fish!

KEEP A WRITTEN RECORD

A written journal will help you to keep track of your fish's quarantine and health record. These records can be invaluable for information on previous treatments, and should include your fish's size, gender, date of purchase and disease history. Also make note of medications used and length of quarantine for each individual aquatic pet.

HOLE IN THE HEAD DISEASE (*HEXAMITA*)

Hole in the head disease is characterized by open sores or whitish pimples on the head and lateral line region. Diseased fish often show a lack of appetite. It is caused by *Hexamita*, an internal parasite. *Hexamita* is a very motile organism with six flagella. It's commonly found in such species as discus, angelfish, cichlids, goldfish and oscars. Some species of marine fish have also been known to be infected with this disease. "The Discus Parasite," as it has been commonly named, can be a serious problem in overstressed discus and angelfish. The organism infects the digestive tract and then moves on to other organs such as the liver and kidneys.

Some theories of contributing factors to this disease are overuse of activated carbon, stray electrical voltage in the water caused by faulty equipment, poor water quality and an improper diet. If this disease goes untreated, it can be fatal or cause permanent deformities. There is no single cause known for this disease, and it's believed that it develops as a result of a convergence of factors.

Treatment—Use Flagyl to remove the pathogen and introduce a varied diet formulated with vitamins and vegetables to help prevent reoccurrence. Water changes can also be effective.

The full finnage shown on this fish would not be apparent in a discus suffering from fin rot.

Fin Rot

Fins and tail erode away or become inflamed due to bacteria known as *Pseudomonas*.

Treatment—Treat fin rot with a proprietary medication and temporarily elevate the water temperature to prevent reoccurrence. To treat bacterial infections, you should treat the fish in a separate quarantine tank with an antibiotic medication. If the fish is still eating properly, introduce medicated food as part of its diet and treatment.

Gill Flukes

A fish with gill flukes will have swollen, reddish gills and accelerated breathing. The afflicted fish may rub its gills on tank decorations or the gravel bed, display loss of motor control and have glazed eyes.

Egg-laying flukes known as *Dactylogridea* release fertilized eggs into the water that develop off of the host fish. The flukes attach themselves to the gills and do massive amounts of damage. Because the fluke eggs are dispersed into the water during reproduction, they can multiply rapidly and cause large amounts of primary as well as secondary bacterial damage.

Gyrodactylus, commonly known as skin flukes, are usually present on the skin but can also infect the gills. An infected fish may have frayed fins with localized hemorrhages and ulcers on its body. A fish that is suffering from a secondary bacterial infection will usually not survive without prompt treatment.

Treatment—Treat afflicted fish with fluke tabs and follow directions closely for adequate dosages to prevent reinfestation. Medications such as formaldehyde work well at recommended dosages, and will usually require two to three treatments separated daily by 50 percent water changes.

Praziquantel is also effective against this disease, and will cause the flukes to spasm with tremors and fall to the tank floor. Performing frequent water changes will remove the fallen flukes. Salt baths or dips are also very effective. Maximum aeration should be used in the quarantine tank.

ICH (WHITE SPOT DISEASE)

Ich is characterized by white crystal-shaped dots that cover the body and make it look like it has been sprinkled with salt. This disease is commonly found in waters that are maintained at an improper temperature, and is caused by the parasite *Ichthyopthirius*.

Treatment—Treat the afflicted fish with a proprietary ich medication. Elevate the water temperature a few degrees to speed up the parasitic cycle during treatment.

Velvet

Velvet is characterized by a white or golden coat of spots on the body and fins. The afflicted fish will often scratch on the substrate and decorations, and have labored respiration.

Treatment—Treat with a commercial velvet medication.

Fungus

Fungus is characterized by white cotton-like growths on the fins and body. Fungus often appears where the slime coat has been damaged.

When using commercial medications, follow the manufacturer's directions, even if your discus appears to be completely healed.

Treatment—Treat with a commercial fungus medication, and spot-treat afflicted areas with gentian violet. Be sure to follow the manufacturer's directions closely. To help the infected fish along, remove any aggressive fin- or tail-nipping fish and perform a 25 percent water change. Methelyene blue may also be used in severe cases.

Swim Bladder Disease

Fish that have swim bladder problems will have trouble staying in an upright position. Bacterial infections or physical blows during handling usually cause swim bladder damage.

Treatment—Treat the afflicted fish with an antibiotic in a shallow hospital tank. If its condition does not improve, destroy it humanely.

Diseases of the Eye

Discus are prone to eye disorders, usually caused by wounds or scratches that have become infected. When purchasing new decorations or substrate, check the edges carefully to make sure that none are jagged. If

103

there are no sharp decorations or equipment in the tank, be on the lookout for aggressive tankmates. Inflamed eyes can usually be treated by using a simple salt bath.

Intestinal Diseases

Usually, the first sign of an intestinal disease is a fatigued fish that expels a white-colored, stringy textured feces. The majority of intestinal illness in aquarium fish is caused by parasites. Weight loss will be evident. Note that Hole in the Head disease mentioned above is also caused by an intestinal parasite.

A Healthy Slime Coat

Have you ever wondered why fish feel slimy when you touch their skin? The smooth texture is due to an important slime coat that is produced by the fish. The slime coat is actually emitted through the skin, and acts as a natural barrier to ward off illness and disease. If the slime coating gets damaged or weakened, it will allow pathogens or parasites to enter into the body of the fish with little resistance.

Help prevent eye injuries by keeping jagged edge decor out of your tank.

One way to maintain a healthy slime coat for your discus is through the use of marine salt, which acts as a tonic or stress relief aid to promote excretion. By using a measurement of one tablespoon of marine salt to each five gallons of water you can help promote a healthier slime coat. Aloe-vera-based products are also known to have a beneficial effect on maintaining a healthy slime coat.

One Good Home Remedy

There is one good home remedy that you can use instead of medications. The old-fashioned salt bath often works well, and will save you money. Salt baths have been proven effective over time to help cure problems such as fungus infestations, ich and several other types of parasites such as gill flukes. Parasites that are submerged in a salt solution will begin to take on water until they burst and fall off. Just add one teaspoon of table salt for each gallon of water that you have in your hospital tank. Continue adding one teaspoon of salt twice a day for the first five or six days. If the infected fish is not completely well by the sixth day, continue to add one teaspoon of salt for another three days.

Coping with Disease, Sickness and Death

Hobbyists often blame themselves when something goes wrong with their aquatic pets. Aquariums are not 100 percent foolproof by any means. Nothing on earth will last forever, and it is the nature of all living things to eventually return to the earth from which they were created. If you can accept the fact that you are a caretaker and not a miracle worker, only then will you be able to cope with the inevitable loss of a favorite pet.

However, you can have control over certain common diseases by offering your fish the best living conditions available. If you can maintain the environment in which they live at optimum standards and meet their requirements on a daily basis, then you should never have to point a finger at yourself and ask the question: "What did I do wrong?"

part four

Beyond the Basics

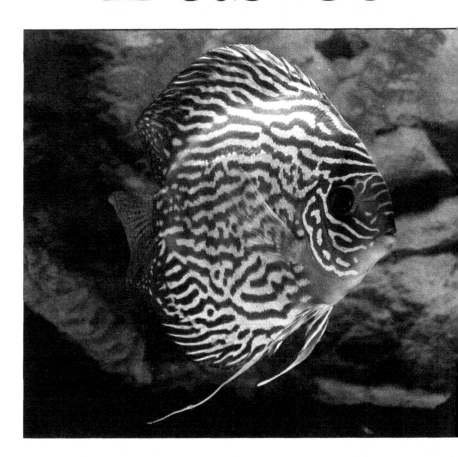

chapter 10

The
Basics
of Breeding

The discus is quickly becoming a favorite species among breeders of tropical freshwater fish. The astounding number of new color varieties has dramatically intensified sales in the past few years. The enjoyment that you will find keeping and successfully breeding the "king" of

freshwater species will provide you with endless hours of pride. Discus breeding is a challenging and fun aspect of aquarium keeping that many new hobbyists are now beginning to achieve on a regular basis.

Reproduction in the Wild

Discus have many natural instincts that cannot easily be removed in captivity. In their native habitat, the rainy season usually begins at the end of November and continues through January. During this period, the water levels increase, and discus begin to spawn. Many discus are trapped in small ponds due to runoff. These small ponds receive a lot of direct sunlight, and very little shade. Temperatures may quickly skyrocket up to 90°F during the breeding season. You'll want to keep these environmental factors in mind when you attempt to breed your discus.

Two Types of Breeding

There are two main techniques that you can use to breed discus. The conventional method involves breeding original strains of discus in order to keep them pure without introducing any type of crossbreeding of domesticated fish. The unconventional method of breeding involves crossing different strains in order to develop new colors.

The conventional method of breeding is much more difficult because wild species of discus frequently carry disease, require optimal water conditions and are generally reluctant to breed in captivity. Tank-bred strains have become accustomed to different types of water parameters and breeding situations, and are much more likely to spawn in the confines of the home aquarium. This type of breeding is usually the best choice for the beginning hobbyist. When breeding, you will have to use a little bit of common sense and plan out your project before choosing spawning pairs. Ruining beautiful strains that have already been developed will not benefit anyone.

> **SETTING THE MOOD**
>
> For spawning purposes, discus like it relatively dark. Lighting in a breeding tank should be kept dim. During spawning, the back of the tank should be covered with a dark background to provide your fish with a sense of security.

Understanding the Natural Process of Breeding

You are the caretaker of the environment in which your fish live. You really have very little impact on the actual breeding process except for offering the proper aquarium conditions. If you understand that your discus are in complete control during spawning and mating rituals, practicing patience will often lead to the best results.

Increasing the Odds

You can increase the odds of a successful spawning by providing the correct water conditions, environment and proper nutrition. Studying the natural environment of the species that you're interested in breeding will give you essential knowledge involved in duplicating conditions that are important during their natural spawning season. Breeding discus is not complicated if you provide the proper conditions and select good breeding stock.

Selecting Spawning Pairs

There are three different schools of thought on selecting spawning partners. (The aquarium hobby is full of dissension, so don't be alarmed.)

Let the Adults Decide

The first method involves purchasing mature adult discus (usually eight or ten) and allowing them time to naturally develop into mated pairs. The drawback to this method is that you are not guaranteed that all off your discus will pair off and become spawning partners.

It is possible (put not probable) that every member of your breeding group will turn out to be all males, or all females. Discus can be very hard to sex properly. But a visual cue can often be seen during the spawning process. The male's reproductive organ protrudes from the lower abdomen and has a very pointed tip on the end. The female's organ also protrudes from the lower abdomen, but it is shaped very much like a straw or tube. This tube is actually a path through which the eggs travel down during spawning. Another way of sexing discus is by observing behavior. The female will usually fan the eggs while the male stands guard over the nest to ward off any would be intruders.

Knowing the sexual identity of your fish will help you to eliminate the possibility of having the same gender of fish in the same tank. Female fish will often lay eggs in the presence of another dominant female who will portray the part of the dominant male. By determining the gender during the first spawning, you can eliminate the guesswork in your breeding schedule.

YOUNG LOVE

The second method that you can use to produce mated pairs is to purchase several smaller-size juveniles and

As juvenile discus mature, they will begin to pair off.

place them in a tank together. As they begin to grow into adults, they will start to pair off (assuming once again that they are not all of the same gender), and the chances are good that you'll obtain at least one breeding pair. Juveniles are usually not as expensive as their adult counterparts.

The best way to determine gender is by waiting for your discus to pair up. Discus are usually sexually mature between the ages of 18 to 24 months. As they grow, a male and female will begin to swim together and stay within close proximity of each other. This behavior is known as pairing off. As the interested parties meet, they will usually have their heads tipped down, their body and fin colors will darken and they'll begin to twitch and dance around each other.

After contact is made, the male of the species will often look for a spawning sight. Common spawning sites include rocks, plants, flat pieces of shale and glass walls. Once he has selected an area, he'll begin to remove debris and clean the site thoroughly.

THE EXPENSIVE APPROACH

One good way to guarantee that you have a compatible spawning couple is to purchase a mated pair. Mated pairs usually consist of two fish that have already spawned, or seem to be moving toward that goal. Note, however, that mated pairs can be very expensive. There is also the possibility that the pair may not mate right away because they have become stressed from transportation.

Selecting Breeding Stock

Whether you select juveniles or adults, always make sure you choose the healthiest specimens that you can find. A healthy discus will have a bright red natural coloration in the eye that circles the pupil of the eyeball. Oversized eyes may be an indication of stunted growth, and fish with overly large eyes should be avoided.

For your breeding stock, look for fish with bright red eyes. These are a sign of good health.

A healthy discus will reproduce at a much faster rate than one that is suffering from illness and disease. Some medications can prolong a fish's ability to reproduce, but may result in sterility. It is always best to begin with healthy specimens, give them quality care, provide a nutritious diet and do frequent water changes to ensure that they remain in top breeding condition. When you are selecting your breeding stock never downplay the importance of a healthy discus, and never settle for second best.

FINS

When choosing your discus, pay special attention to proper fin structure. Make sure that the fish's fins are not torn or ragged, and are in proportion with the body's size. Huge fins often indicate poor inbreeding.

KIDS ON ONE SIDE, ADULTS ON THE OTHER

Juveniles and adults should never be mixed together in a breeding tank. Many hobbyists believe that adult discus can secrete a hormone into the water that can stunt a juvenile's growth. Larger adult discus can also become quite aggressive toward juveniles during the spawning season, so it is best to keep them separated.

The Breeding Tank

The size of your breeding tank will depend on how many discus you're planning to stock. When definite pairs have been formed, they can be relocated to their own spawning tank. A breeding tank will allow them to have their own private area for courting and spawning without being interrupted by other tankmates. A 20- or 30-gallon tank will work well for most individual discus pairs.

WATER CONDITIONS FOR BREEDING

When breeding discus, crystal-clear water conditions should be maintained at all times by performing frequent water changes. A low, acidic pH level of 5.5 to 6.0 should be offered and maintained. Using rainwater, natural peat, chemicals, an ion exchanger or a reverse osmosis unit can soften the pH. With the aforementioned water conditions, the female can easily deposit her eggs without any complications.

The temperature range should be kept at a constant level between 84° to 86°F. Some hobbyists prefer to provide a higher temperature of 90° to 92°F. However, the higher temperatures will create a lower oxygen level in the water. Conditions can also be jeopardized at these higher temperatures due to the inability of beneficial bacteria to grow properly. You'll need sufficient bacteria to filter the water efficiently.

FILTRATION

One of the best filtration methods that can be used for breeding discus is an economical sponge filter. Sponge filters are readily available at most pet supply shops and actually serve three purposes in the breeding tank.

1. A sponge filter will serve as a biological medium and will provide aeration to create mild water flow.

2. Free-swimming fry cannot be harmed or sucked into a sponge unit as is often the case with a power filter.

3. Sponges also serve as a feeding station of fine food particles for the baby fry.

> ### EGG EATERS
>
> If the eggs are not fertilized, they are often eaten. This event may occur if both fish are female (two females have been known to pair up), or if the male is sterile or not mature enough to breed. There are also cases where the parents begin to eat the eggs after they are laid for no apparent reason. If one parent is a constant egg eater, try pairing it with another mate, or dropping it from your breeding program.

If you do decide to use a power filter or other fast-flowing unit, make sure that the intake tube is covered with a small piece of panty hose (held on by a rubber band) so that the fry cannot be sucked up into it.

WATER ADDITIVES

Black water extracts offer trace minerals that are found in the fish's natural Amazonian habitat. Black water extracts will also help to maintain proper body color and a natural soft water environment.

Some hobbyists and breeders use the extracts as a spawning aid, but they are not necessary.

DECORATIONS FOR SPAWNING

A female discus usually prefers to lay her eggs on a vertical surface. Much like her native cousin the angelfish, the discus will spawn on a wide leaf, a clay pot, a flat

Here, discus fry cling to a rock placed in a vertical position inside the tank.

rock, a breeding cone or a plastic PVC pipe. Discus breeding cones are often used by professional breeders, and can be ordered through mail-order houses or found at high-quality pet shops. Make sure that any decorations that you use for breeding purposes are thoroughly cleaned and sanitized before they're added to the tank.

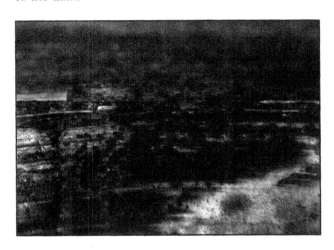

CONDITIONING THE BREEDING PAIR

A healthy diet is very importance to the breeding cycle. Healthy fish produce more eggs than those who suffer from illness or malnutrition. About two weeks prior to spawning activities, start feeding your pair live foods such as brine shrimp and insect larvae.

Most fish reproduce in cycles that can be tracked by maintaining a written record of dates and times of previous spawning activities. Some pairs have been known to reproduce every two weeks. A breeding journal will give you a good idea of when to start your conditioning methods. Your fish should always be kept in top condition, but live foods offered prior to breeding will help to boost their vitality and health for spawning, which involves the use of a lot of physical energy.

Frequent water changes will also help to condition your discus for spawning, by imitating the natural rainy season during which they breed in the wild.

The Spawning Process

The first signs of spawning usually begin when a pair of discus court each other by swimming side by side. Occasional the lovebirds will playfully nip at each other, or swim around in circles. The most relevant spawning sign to watch for is the cleaning of a potential breeding site by the male of the species. After a suitable spot has been chosen, the female will often help him with his housecleaning duties.

When the female has become satis-fied with a cleaned area, she'll begin to make a few "test runs." Afterward, she will deposit her eggs while the male follows close behind fertilizing each one.

Depending on her size and health, the female discus will lay between 50 and 400 eggs during one spawn-ing session. This entire process usually takes about an hour to accomplish. After the eggs have been deposited and fertilized by the male, the female will then care

> ### FIVE IMPORTANT BREEDING TIPS
>
> 1. Be patient—allow nature to run its course.
>
> 2. Keep the water's pH level low, and the temperature warm for best results.
>
> 3. Make sure that you obtain a compatible pair that are of breeding age.
>
> 4. Provide a secluded area for spawning without interruptions from other species.
>
> 5. Condition your discus for breeding with a varied diet consisting of live foods.

for the eggs through a process known as "fanning." The female will hover over the nest area and begin to move her fins in a rapid manner in order to create a water flow over the eggs. Fanning will remove any sed-iment or fine particles on the eggs to prevent the nest from becoming contaminated with debris, and will help to ward off fungus invasion.

HATCHING

The first signs of hatching should be visible within seventy-two hours from the time the eggs are laid. At this time, the female may move the eggs to another site within the tank to provide a cleaner area for the eggs until they reach the free-swimming stage. Both parents are responsible for brood care and are usually known to be very attentive caretakers.

FEEDING THE BABIES

For the first three to four days after hatching, the fry will receive all of their nutrition from the eggs' yolk sacs, which remain attached to their bodies. During this time, they will stay in the nest area and are not capable of swimming.

As they become stronger and begin to swim on their own, they'll then travel away from the nest and move closer to the parent fish where they will be supplied food through a skin secretion known as discus milk. At this point, it is best to leave the fry with the parents for at least a week so that they can receive plenty of the nutritional food that is being supplied through the mucus coat.

The young fry derive nutrition by consuming discus milk that is secreted through the parent's skin.

When the fry begin to eat other foods, such as live baby brine shrimp or finely crushed flake food, they can then be separated from the parents and placed in their own grow-out tank. The grow-out tank should be completely cycled and contain the same water conditions as the breeding tank to prevent transportation shock.

RAISING THE FRY ARTIFICIALLY

Some hobbyists prefer to raise discus eggs by removing them from the parents after they are fertilized. The young feed on a paste made out of dried eggs, which is spread around the edge of a shallow pan. Water must be changed after every feeding. The advantage to using this method is that more fry are usually raised to adulthood. Unfortunately, artificial methods tend to encourage production of genetically neglectful parents, which would not survived in the wild. This process demands a lot of time and attention, and is really not recommended for inexperienced discus breeders.

Breeding Choices

When breeding discus, there are no set boundaries or guidelines. Many techniques and different ideas have already been developed, tried, tested and proven with successful results. Crossbreeding, inbreeding and genetic manipulation have been introduced by professional breeders to create a wide variety of new strains and color patterns. Some experienced hobbyists still choose to breed only the original strains of discus in order to keep their genetics pure.

The various options and choices that you may want to implement into your own breeding program are up to you, and should be based upon the goals that you personally wish to achieve. The main goal, of course, is to have fun with your personal breeding project. If breeding becomes tiresome or frustrating, give it a rest. Come back to it when you're in a more positive frame of mind.

MEETING MARKET DEMAND IN YEARS PAST
In the earlier days of fish keeping, the retail discus market contained only the natural wild species, which were somewhat bland in appearance. Retailers (to meet the increasing public interest and demand) began massive breeding programs in order to flood the market with many different colors and attractive strains.

CROSSBREEDING AND INBREEDING

Crossbreeding and inbreeding often raises eyebrows among conservationists. Many people believe that the original strains from the Amazon region that were first captured and introduced into the hobby should be kept pure and never be crossbred or inbred. Other hobbyists believe that the efforts put forth in acquiring new strains through captive breeding have produced stronger and more beautiful species that can be appreciated by current and future fish keepers alike.

ARTIFICIAL COLORING

In order to meet the demand for striking discus, a few unscrupulous dealers began using hormones and dyes for artificial color enhancements. Red brine shrimp, which have the potential to create temporary red coloration, were also fed in massive amounts. Fortunately, most dealers do not use these deceptive practices. Discus that have been artificially colored will often have an orange tint around their eyes, mouth and pectoral fins.

THE FAILURES OF UNCONVENTIONAL BREEDING

Crossbreeding and inbreeding of different species have produced so many new color varieties that they have nearly eliminated the temptation to add any type of chemicals, foods or color additives to create a more desirable looking fish. But through the years, several strains were developed that were noted to be prone to diseases, have disfigured bodies, oversized fins and many other unpleasant physical features. Some of the new strains were not consistently capable of reproducing new offspring, which indicated that the entire breeding and culling process had not been fully developed. Today, these poor strains of discus are becoming a rarity.

THE SUCCESSES OF UNCONVENTIONAL BREEDING

Many strains of discus have been developed that are capable of reproducing hardy and disease-resistant young. Many discus are capable of producing true offspring such as the Pigeon Blood, the Blue Diamond and the Turquoise strains. Without the use of unconventional breeding practices being implemented by professional breeders, the selection and variety of discus would still be somewhat limited today.

Crossbreeding can produce positive results such as a new color form, better body shape, positive fin structure and even a better overall appearance in the body of a discus. A breeder who wishes to be successful in developing a new color will have to be creative and experiment with crossbreeding several different strains.

Instructions on how to create new colors are not usually freely offered and remain top trade secrets among serious breeders. There is still a high demand for a new top-quality strain of fish. This demand creates a very competitive market, so don't be offended if a breeder refuses to let you in on his best secrets.

Development of Popular Hybrid Strains

Not all crosses are a trade secret!

BLUE DIAMOND DISCUS

The Blue Diamond discus was originally developed by crossing a Blue Turquoise with a Cobalt Blue. Select offspring that possessed a desirable solid blue body color were then crossed with the albino discus to produce the red eyes that are present in the Blue Diamonds. This new strain is a very successful breeder, and will produce true offspring.

RED ROYAL BLUE TURQUOISE DISCUS

Crossbreeding the Red Turquoise with the Blue Turquoise resulted in a highly colored mixture of the two.

RED SNAKESKIN DISCUS

This discus was developed by crossing Green and Blue Snakeskins that had a reddish base with a Red

Turquoise that possessed fine bodylines. The redder discus from the offspring are then selected and cross-bred with each other to create the Red Snakeskin appearance.

Breeders cross-bred different fish to create Blue Diamond discus, which now produce true offspring.

THE MARLBORO RED DISCUS

The Marlboro Red discus was developed by crossbreeding the Pigeon Blood with a Brown discus. The base body color is orange, which is then covered with a patch of golden red.

Keeping Discus Pure

There is a moral and scientific need to keep any species in its pure form in case it should ever become endangered or threatened with extinction. A beginner who is just starting out should avoid trying to crossbreed or inbreed any forms of discus unless they are educated in genetics. A beginning breeder should work at breeding within the same strains before attempting to try the more advanced stages of crossing other strains.

FISH PRODUCED IN CAPTIVITY

There are plenty of captive-bred tropical fish available to hobbyists. Buying captive-bred species lessens the need for collectors to continually interfere with the natural Amazonian environment. Some methods of capture are noted to be inhumane and leave irreversible effects on the natural ecological systems in which these fish are often taken. Purchasing only tank-raised fish, whether they are original species or newly created colors, should be an important part of every hobbyist's goal in helping to protect the natural environment.

Obtaining Breeder Points

If you're fortunate enough to be a member of a tropical fish club that awards points for your breeding efforts, you'll have a good reason to try working with different species. Many clubs offer the needed information and paperwork for you to become involved in a licensed breeder program. Several different types of fish may have to bred in order to receive the required minimal points to be licensed. You can obtain any needed guidelines or information through your local fish club if they support this type of breeding program. If you're not a member of a club or want to find one in your area, you may want check the Internet or inquire at your local pet supply shop.

chapter 11

Resources

Magazines

In order to keep up with rapidly changing equipment, organizations, health and breeding technology, beginning hobbyists can read aquarium magazines to supply them with current information. The following list of magazines will give you good ideas and insights into the aquarium hobby. You will also find many articles, club information and discus retailers in all of these publications.

Practical Fishkeeping Magazine, ℅ Motorsport, RR 1, Box 200 D, Jonesburg, MO 63351; phone (314) 488-3113.

Tropical Fish Hobbyist, One Neptune Plaza. Neptune City, NJ 07753; phone (908) 988-8400

Freshwater and Marine Aquarium Magazine, P.O. Box 487, Sierra Madre, CA 91024

Aquarium Fish Magazine, PO Box 6040, Mission Viejo, CA 92690; phone (949) 855-8822

Books

Alderton, David. *The Complete Idiot's Guide to Tropical Aquarium Fish Care.* New York: Howell Book House, 1998.

Axelrod, Herbert R. *Dr. Axelrod's Mini Atlas*. Neptune City, NJ: TFH Publications Inc., 1995.

Bailey, M., and G. Sandford. *The New Guide to Aquarium Fish*. London: Hermes House, 1998.

Braemer, H., and I. Scheurmann. *Tropical Fish*. Hauppauge, NY: Barron's Educational Series Inc., 1983.

Cacutt, Len. *Natures Facts, Fishes*. London: Grange Books Limited, 1992.

Cohen, Sylvan, M.D. *Prevention and Care of Tropical Fish Diseases*. Harrison, NJ: The Pet Library Ltd, 1972.

Dawes, John. *Tropical Aquarium Fish*. Avenel, New York: Crescent Books, 1996.

Keller, Gunter. *Discus*. Neptune City, NJ: TFH Publications Inc., 1976.

Mills, Dick. *101 Essential Tips, Aquarium Fish*. New York: DK Publishing, Inc., 1996.

———. *You and Your Aquarium*. New York: Alfred A. Knopf, Inc., 1986.

Scheurmann, Ines. *Aquarium Fish Breeding*. Hauppauge, NY: Barron's Educational Series Inc., 1990.

Scott, Peter. *The Complete Aquarium*. New York: Alfred A. Knopf, Inc., 1991.

Skomal, Gregory. *Setting Up a Freshwater Aquarium*. New York: Howell Book House, 1997.

Sweeney, Mary. *The Cichlid: An Owner's Guide to a Happy Healthy Pet*. NY: Howell Book House, 1999.

Tetra/Second Nature. *Digest For The Successful Aquarium*. Melle, Germany: Tetra Press, 1994.

Wardley Corporation. *Fin Facts*. Secaucus, NJ: Wardley Corporation, 1992.

Zupanc, Gunter K.H. *Fish and Their Behavior*. Melle, Germany: Tetra Press, 1985

Zurlo, Georg. *Cichlids*. English translation: Hauppauge, NY: Barron's Educational Series, Inc., 1991.

Internet Links

There are many Web sites that can provide you with discus information and help you learn more about your new pet. The following Web sites are loaded with helpful information, purchasing sites and also provide several other useful discus links.

DISCUS ON THE WEB:

Dan's Tropical Kings
http://www.tdnet.com/%7Etropical/
TROPIC5&E1.HTM

The Discus Place—Quality Discus at a Fair Price
http://members.aol.com/discusplaz/discus.html

Jack Wattley Discus
http://www.wattleydiscus.com/

The Discus Connection
http://members.aol.com/discusconn/

The Discus Page
http://www.ee.pdx.edu/~davidr/

The Discus Breeders Website
http://www.info.clio.it/cultura/associazione/

Bing Seto's Discus World Homepage
http://www.discusworld.com

The Cichlid Room Companion—Breeding Discus
http://www2.cichlidae.com/cichlidroom/articles/
a015.html

Clubs and Organizations

Fish clubs and organizations are a great way to learn more about discus care, and to communicate with other hobbyists who share your interests on fish keeping, health and welfare. This list will provide you with a good starting point for finding a local club near you. Most of these organizations will be able to give you information on discus organizations near your hometown.

Discus Club (Singapore)
Box 722 Clementi West Street 2#01-162
Singapore 120722

North American Discus Society
Contact Bob Wilson
6939 Justine Drive
Mississauga, ON
Canada L4T 1M4

International Aquarium Society
P.O. Box 373
Maine, NY 13802-0373

British Discus Association
Contact BDA
c/o F.W. Ashworth
41 Pengwern
Llangollen, Clwyd. LL20 8AT
England

American Cichlid Society
P.O. Box 5351
Naperville, IL 60567

Fish Shows

Entering a fish show can be a great way for you to expand your fish-keeping skills, win prizes and display your aquarium keeping and breeding skills. When you enter or attend a fish show, you'll be able to find many aquarium fish experts who will be more than happy to answer any questions that you may have concerning your discus.

Breeding, raising and preparing discus for competition will also help to improve your aquarium-keeping skills. Only top-quality livestock is entered in fish competitions, so you'll need to do a lot of research and work on water conditions, nutrition and discus health in order to have a competitive entry.

Most fish shows are organized by aquarium societies. These aquatic societies are often sponsored by local clubs and groups for fun and social gatherings, or they may be international in scope and have thousands of entries.